ESCAPE
from
IDI
AMIN'S
SLAUGHTERHOUSE

ESCAPE
from
IDI
AMIN'S
SLAUGHTERHOUSE

Wycliffe Kato

Quartet Books
London   New York

First published by Quartet Books Limited 1989
A member of the Namara Group
27/29 Goodge Street
London W1P 1FD

Copyright © Wycliffe Kato 1989

An earlier and shorter
version of this narrative first
appeared in *Granta*, 22, Autumn 1987

British Library Cataloguing in Publication Data

Kato, Wycliffe, *1940–*
   Escape from Idi Amin's slaughterhouse.
   1. Uganda. Social life. Biographies
   I. Title
967.6'104'0924

ISBN 0 7043 2706 6

Typeset by MC Typeset Limited, Gillingham
Printed and bound in Great Britain by
The Camelot Press plc. Southampton

Dedicated to
the memory of Warrant Officer II John Okech
who died so we could live

ACKNOWLEDGEMENTS

To Edmée Frans of Nairobi and Thierry Konietzko of
Montreal for invaluable help with the manuscript

and

Susan Yorke, for warm support and admirable editing

Contents

PART THREE   GOAL ATTAINED

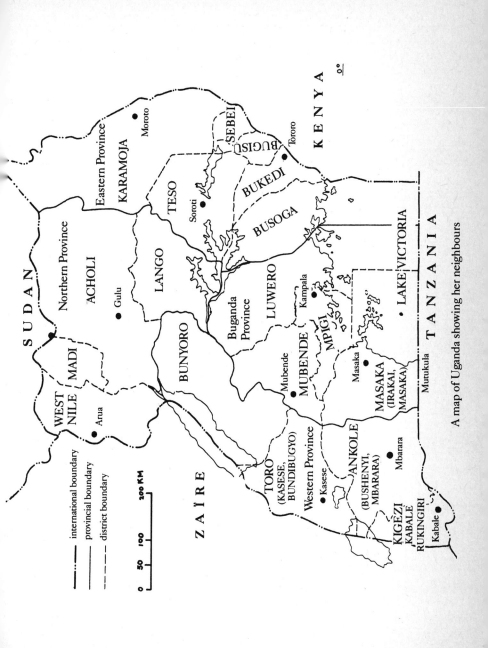

A map of Uganda showing her neighbours

1

INTRODUCTION

'This is how I imagined Heaven to be!' exclaimed the Director of Civil Aviation of Niger, a Sahelian country, on discovering Uganda, where he had come to attend a meeting.

Winston Churchill called it the Pearl of Africa. Indeed, it is a lush country, blessed with plentiful rains and an even equatorial climate, so that the rich red soil produces food in abundance. The rolling hills are always green, covered with coffee bushes, mango trees, banana plantations and other food crops. The neat houses of the smallholders are scattered around the countryside, each surrounded by a cluster of banana trees which can feed the family for many years if properly cared for. The cash crops – coffee and cotton – provide the money for clothing and school fees.

Of course, this applies essentially to Buganda, the ancient kingdom which gave its name to the country. As long ago as the end of the last century, the Baganda (the people of Buganda) gave up manual labour to seek employment in Kampala, hiring people from western Uganda (Ankole) and Rwanda to cultivate the soil. No wonder that the British relied essentially on them to administer the country and they became the backbone of the civil service.

When Uganda gained independence in 1962, it was a prosperous country. The economy, based on agriculture, was buoyant. There was a small but growing industrial sector, especially after the completion of the Owen Falls hydro-electric scheme at Jinja.

The country had an extensive network of paved roads and a good health service with several hundred rural dispensaries, numerous hospitals and an excellent hospital in Kampala (Mulago). There were outstanding institutions of learning, including the well-known University of Makerere.

Alas, all this promise was shattered by political instability due to tribal and regional tensions. Uganda has a large number of tribes and also, like most former colonies, has boundaries which are so artificial that almost all around they bisect tribes. Apart from considerable tribal cultural differences, Uganda has clearly marked ethnic groupings which are even geographically separated. You have the Nilotics who occupy the northern part of the country and the Bantus who dominate the western, southern, and a big part of the eastern part of Uganda. The differences between the two groupings are not just in the language and culture, but also in several other areas. In fact, this country which was so blessed by nature is composed of so many tribes and ethnic groupings that it would be very difficult to find a true nationalist, one who would not initially look for his tribal support in order to achieve his political objective, which in most cases would not basically be for the nation but for his own personal gain.

At the time of independence, tribes had not all reached the same level of social and economic development. Some were organized in monarchies: Bunyoro, Toro and Ankole in the west, Buganda and Busoga in the central part. In the more arid north lived the Nilotic tribes, the Acholi and the Langi, who formed a majority in the army, and the Nilo-Hamitic tribes, Teso and Karamojong, who were cattle herders. The Sudan-oriented (Lugbara, Madi, Kakwa) in the north-west had not made much progress, having no social structure above the village level.

The Baganda were the most numerous (today they number eighteen per cent of a population of fourteen million) and had the most elaborate political and administrative structure. At the top was the king, the Kabaka, who was the head of all the clans. The loyalty of the subjects was assured by the king marrying into as many clans as possible. It was enhanced by the practice by which all kings belonged to their mother clan, so that there was no royal clan, since every clan was free to offer wives to the king, and most did.

The Buganda Agreement of 1900 placed the Kabaka under the protection of the British Crown. It legalized ownership of most of the land by the Kabaka and about 3,700 nobles; it also freed the slaves. Prior to this agreement, all land in Buganda belonged to the Kabaka, who allocated some of it to his subordinates as he wished. By this agreement, land was distributed to the Kabaka, members of the royal family and the chiefs, while the remainder was reserved for the British Crown, as was the case for the rest of the country. Apart from the land reserved for the British Crown, which was known as public land, the rest was private and came to be known as *mailo* land because of the mispronunciation of the word 'mile' by the Baganda. Proper land titles were given to owners. Later, private land changed ownership as time went on; this gave an opportunity to more and more peasants to buy land. The agreement helped to shape Buganda into a country of smallholdings and prevented the white settlers from coming as they came to Kenya and Rhodesia.

Uganda became independent on 9 October 1962, but negotiations had been going on for two years before, so deep were the divisions. The problems were of such an emotional nature that the British Government was urged to solve them before independence. Buganda wanted separate independence, and the first constitution drafted for the new republic was of a federal nature, allowing the traditional kingdoms to retain their autonomy. Some claim that this concession to self-government was a crucial error, as it prevented the formation of a strong centralized government.

In addition to the issue of Buganda separation, there was the antagonism between Protestants and Catholics. Every district was divided along religious lines. The division ran through the school system, since schools were run by missionaries, and was reflected in the political parties. The Democratic Party (DP) was Catholic and leftist, whereas the Kabaka Yekka and the Uganda People's Congress (UPC) were Protestant, the former being conservative. The Protestants, who had been dominant in all spheres of political life for the sixty years preceding independence, feared that they might lose their supremacy and were opposed to the DP.

The first general elections which brought internal self-government to Uganda were won by the Democratic Party, led by Benedicto Kiwanuka, a devout Roman Catholic and a Muganda. However, the Baganda had boycotted these elections and because of this Obote, the leader of the UPC, persuaded the British Government to have another general election within a matter of months. Obote outwitted Benedicto Kiwanuka by allying his UPC party with Kabaka Yekka, forming an alliance which was later exposed as a 'marriage of convenience', to get the Baganda's support which Obote considered essential for him in order to fulfil his ambition to be President of Uganda. Incidentally, possibly by coincidence, he took a Muganda as his wife at about the same time.

The alliance won the elections and Obote was called upon by the governor to form a government. Therefore Apollo Milton Obote, a Langi from the north, became prime minister, while the king of the most powerful and populous kingdom, Sir Edward Mutesa II, was made the president of the new nation.

However, the alliance was short-lived, and in May 1966 Obote deposed the king, who fled to exile in London where he was to die. Obote called his army chief, Idi Amin, to put down the ensuing Baganda rebellion and the overzealous Amin completely destroyed the Kabaka's palace. Obote turned the ruin into a military barracks while the rest of the kingdom's government buildings were turned into military headquarters. This earned Obote the hostility of most Baganda, and they never became reconciled with him.

During the next five years, following the abrogation of the 1962 constitution, the country had a quasi-military regime. Obote took over the office of president and ruled through corruption, nepotism and tribalism, thereby accentuating the existing divisions.

By manipulating the civil service and local government, he undermined the stability of the administration. By unjustified promotions, transfers, etc., he destroyed the integrity and morale

xiv

of the state employees. He tampered with the judicial system and redrew district, provincial and council boundaries, destroying the faith of the people in the government's impartiality. Amin was later to complete this task of destruction.

What led to Obote's fall was his involvement in the reorganization of the army. On 25 January 1971, he was deposed by Amin while attending a Commonwealth summit in Singapore. Hysterical crowds rejoiced in the streets of Kampala, little knowing how they were going to suffer under the new ruler. In his nine years of power, Amin succeeded in wrecking the economy and murdered hundreds of thousands of people. Educated Ugandans, who were particularly exposed to his ire, left in large numbers, depriving the country of its élite.

Although Amin ruled through terror with the help of the State Research Bureau, the army and the police, he had local supporters — big businessmen and some civil servants — and foreign benefactors who helped him to consolidate his position. British, Americans and Kenyans continued to be coffee buyers, the latter selling the coffee which was smuggled out of Uganda. In addition, Kenya found in Uganda an outlet for its own industrial products after the decline of Ugandan industry precipitated by the expulsion of the Asian community in 1972 (Amin's so-called 'economic war'). The Russians and French supplied arms. East Germans trained the State Research Bureau staff, notably in telecommunications. The British provided aid for training the army and the intelligence service. Israel carried out large construction projects and supplied aircraft and aviation equipment. Pakistan sent technical personnel to replace the expelled Asians (mostly Indians).

These dealings were so profitable that some of them went on until the last days of Amin's regime.

And yet inside the country, the economy declined tragically. Cash crops were abandoned, having become unprofitable because prices fixed by the government were never raised, and people returned to subsistence agriculture. Essential commodities like cooking oil, salt, sugar and soap became pathetically rare.

There were many attempts to overthrow Amin, both from

within and from outside the country, but all failed. The internal resistance was passive, taking the form of church attendance.

It took an eight-month war by 45,000 Tanzanians and 2,000 Ugandan liberation soldiers, led by Oyite Ojok and Museveni, to topple Amin. The hostilities were launched by Amin himself. In October 1978, in an attempt to regain control over his army, whom he had vainly tried to purge once more of suspicious elements, Amin created a diversion by invading Tanzania in the Kagera Salient, in the south-west. Surprisingly, in view of the longstanding hostility between the two governments, the border was poorly defended and the Ugandan army occupied the area easily, looting, raping and killing at whim. Tanzania was forced to mobilize the Tanzanian People's Defence Force to push the Ugandan soldiers back. In January 1979, Tanzanian forces crossed the Ugandan border. Uganda's liberation war had started. The Tanzanians cleansed the country systematically of Amin's soldiers, most of whom simply ran away, abandoning arms and ammunition in large quantities.

In the meantime, a government in exile was formed at the Moshi Unity Conference, in Tanzania. Professor Yusufu Lule, an elderly soft-spoken Muganda, was chosen to head the caretaker government, being considered an ideal compromise candidate between the various groups of the coalition, a good number of which Obote was controlling remotely from his exile home in Dar es Salaam and most likely through Nyerere's hotlines in the State House.

Lule stayed in power for only sixty-eight days, his autocratic ways having alienated many non-Baganda. Another widely supported reason is that he tried to steer his government independent of Tanzania, which immensely displeased Nyerere and Obote, and he had to go. In fact, from Entebbe International Airport, he was flown straight to Dar es Salaam, where he was kept in Nyerere's State House like a prisoner (incommunicado) until Nyerere gave in to international pressure to let him be taken for medical treatment, which he received in London, where he remained in exile until his death.

Lule was replaced by Godfrey Lukongwas Binaisa, QC, also a Muganda. He had returned just like any other exile from New York, where he had been practising law. The appointment surprised not only most Ugandans, but even Binaisa himself. Again, there was some indication of Obote's remote control of the government in Uganda through Nyerere's hotline from Dar es Salaam.

Binaisa, having been a staunch supporter of Obote, and having been the author of Obote's infamous 'pigeon-hole constitution' which legalized Obote's usurping of power by military force in 1966, was for a long time at great pains to convince Ugandans that he was not there as Obote's puppet. (After deposing Sir Edward Mutesa II as president, Obote had a new constitution drafted. He directed all members of parliament by radio to find copies of the new constitution, which they were expected to adopt the following afternoon, in their pigeon holes. It was this 1967 constitution which formed the basis for the dictatorial rule which has caused all the sufferings of Ugandans.)

Binaisa tried, like Lule, to reshuffle the cabinet without consulting the National Consultative Council formed at Moshi as an interim parliament, and he was ousted in a rapid coup after having made the blunder of transferring Obote's number-one supporter and chief architect, and also a relative, Oyite Ojok, from the post of army chief of staff to that of an ambassador.

Under Binaisa, insecurity and killings in and around Kampala became rife. No real explanation has been given for this gun rule. During Amin's regime, courts and police had lost their *raison d'être*, and people had become used to resolving their differences with a bullet. It was easy to find a killer for a small reward, as Tanzanian and Ugandan soldiers were poorly paid, if at all. People had helped themselves to the arms left behind by Amin's troops and used them for stealing. The economy was in a mess. The currency was worthless and the black market was the only real one.

A military commission then took over. It was headed by Paulo Muwanga, a very staunch supporter of Obote, Oyite Ojok and

Yoweri Museveni. The commission was strongly suspected of finally paving the way for Obote's return to power as President of Uganda. Indeed, he not only came back in May 1980, but was made president after the much-disputed elections of December that same year. During their whole period in office, Paulo Muwanga and all the military forces, led by Oyite Ojok, gave clear indications that they were supporting Obote's return to office. Justice Wambuzi was abruptly replaced by Justice Masika as the country's chief justice before the general elections. This move was strongly suspected to ensure UPC legal (or better still, illegal) backing in case election disputes were taken to courts of law. As if all this were not enough, Muwanga, as chairman of the military commission, hurriedly passed a decree making it illegal for anybody (including the chairman of the electoral commission) to publish election results except himself.

The offence was punishable by a fine of Uganda Shillings 500,000 (approximately £5,000) or five years' imprisonment, or both. The timing of the decree was so spectacular that it required a Queen's Counsel to clear the doubts in people's minds concerning its genuineness. It was made while crowds were already rejoicing, having 'misheard' some foreign radio stations report that the Democratic Party had won the majority of the seats.

After it was announced that Obote's party, the UPC, had defeated the Baganda-dominated Democratic Party of Ssemogerere, as well as Museveni's Uganda Patriotic Movement, both complained immediately of ballot-rigging. The elections had been observed by a Commonwealth team, which declared them valid, in spite of various irregularities. It is true that the population had been able to go to the polling stations in large numbers, delighted at the chance to express their views after so many years of dictatorship, but the counting was disputed.

Museveni rejected Obote's legitimacy and launched a guerrilla campaign which became the justification of a new reign of terror. Under the pretext of fighting the 'bandits', as the rebels were called, the army pillaged the civilian population. To prevent the people from helping the guerrillas, Obote detained thousands of civilians in camps, where they died from torture, hunger and disease. Amnesty International published a strongly-worded report giving details of systematic torture and killings of civilians by the Ugandan army. In a pastoral letter published a few days before Obote was deposed for the second time, Cardinal Nsubuga wrote: 'Since Obote was elected in December 1980, Ugandans of all political factions have been killed. There is not a single Ugandan who has not lost a relative or a close friend. There are innumerable widows and orphans everywhere in the country.'

A turning point in Obote's regime came with the death of Oyite Ojok, the army chief of staff, who was killed in December 1983 in a helicopter crash. He was the only one who could control the soldiers and he was trusted by Obote, coming from the same tribe and being a relative. Obote hesitated for nine months before replacing him, not knowing whether he could trust the more senior officers, who were Acholi, or whether he should promote a more junior one from his tribe, the Langi. He finally opted for the latter solution, which was to prove his undoing.

The discipline and morale of the army continued to deteriorate, and Museveni's guerrillas extended their activities to the west, capturing Fort Portal in July 1985. The shoot-outs between Acholi and Langi in the barracks over promotions signalled Obote's end. On 27 July, General Tito Okello, an Acholi, marched with his troops from Gulu, in the north, to Kampala without any resistance from the government forces and announced that Obote was overthrown. That very day, the deposed president had crossed the border into Kenya early in the morning, accompanied by some members of his cabinet. He is accused of having seized the foreign-currency reserves of the Central Bank before leaving the country. He has now taken refuge in Zambia.

Uganda has suffered under civil rule as well as under military regimes. Its people have not enjoyed their independence because of a few individuals whose determination to remain in power irrespective of the mandate of Ugandans has turned them into dictators. Nevertheless, one can only hope that the miseries of the Ugandan people will come to an end and that Ugandans will be able to live in peace and freedom again.*

* *Since this book was written President Yoweri Museveni has come to power and has been able to restore law and order throughout most of the country, notably the most densely settled areas.*

PART ONE

IT CAN HAPPEN HERE

1

THE DREADED STATE
RESEARCH BOYS

People called it incredible, newspapers dubbed it 'the Famous Nakasero Escape', international radio stations referred to it as an unprecedented escape, 'better than those of World War II'. I called it a miracle. Even now I still wonder how we managed to escape from Idi Amin's slaughterhouse, Nakasero Prison, and survive.

Nakasero was the headquarters of Amin's infamous State Research Bureau. This was his most trusted and useful department, next to the army, as it was the one he used to ensure his survival. It was therefore understandably the most feared organization in his regime. Its purpose was to eliminate, by the most brutal methods possible, all Amin's enemies. It is difficult to categorize Amin's enemies as most of them were imaginary. Nevertheless, there were several organizations both in the country and outside whose members were plotting to assassinate him. There was also a potential threat to his well-being from a growing number of prosperous and popular figures, intellectuals, politicians and civil servants, who were finding it difficult to keep abreast of Amin's policies because of the conflicting statements made by him or on his behalf by his 'military spokesman'.

The State Research Bureau infiltrated every corner of the country and performed its elimination duties so well that husbands stopped discussing Uganda's political affairs with their wives, or friends with each other. It consisted mainly of Amin's tribesmen, the Kakwas, a very small tribe in the north-western corner of Uganda. Amin made certain that Kakwas held all top positions everywhere, from the civil service to the Church.

Unfortunately for him, the Kakwas were not only one of the most insignificant tribes numerically but were also hopelessly backward. Amin realized he had to cross the tribal border to secure the help of more advanced sister tribes such as the Lugbaras, the Madis and others — but always restricting himself to his district of West Nile. Even then the number was insufficient; there were just too many positions to fill. Accordingly he enlisted Nubians from southern Sudan across the international border.

Nubians are a large tribe and, as a good number had settled in Uganda — mainly in the Bombo area — after the Second World War, they proved invaluable as they fitted well in Kakwa circles. Because they were also fluent in most local languages, they were extremely useful in the State Research Bureau's particular work of collecting information and then eliminating those reported on.

According to one particular story, Amin himself was a Nubian but had to claim to be a Kakwa so that he could pose as a Ugandan. As his parents were settled in Bombo, there may be some truth in this. Furthermore, from the beginning of his regime, Nubians enjoyed special treatment and being a Nubian was an excellent recommendation for an influential job in the country. As a result, all small tribes whose members could pass as Nubians, particularly in the West Nile, took advantage of the situation. The official medium of communication of the State Research Bureau was Nubian. Although Amin later recruited from all tribes, he always made certain that only those who could speak Nubian were put in controlling positions. Consequently the word Nubian became synonymous with State Research, just as State Research was synonymous with killing.

State Research boys specialized in merciless killings, of babies and pregnant women as well as aged and helpless men, mostly totally innocent. State Research boys were generally very young, between eighteen and twenty-five, and because of their youth they killed as a means of enriching themselves. Their most

4

common method was kidnapping: the victim was killed, the body thrown where it could not be found and then a demand for money was made to the relatives of the deceased. This came to be known as 'disappearance'.

People disappeared from offices, cinemas, highways, homes, etc. In many cases they were merely kidnapped, while in others smartly-dressed personnel would pose as Amin's messengers sent to collect someone 'wanted by the president'. Everyone in Uganda feared the State Research boys, and it was common knowledge that those taken by them never returned.

Another dirty game played by these boys was to cheat the relatives of their victims of colossal sums of ransom money on the pretence that the victim would be released. This is what made the bureau so attractive to a certain type of young man or woman.

Nakasero was the headquarters of the State Research Bureau and, as such, Amin's principal slaughterhouse. Very few survived Nakasero – being taken there was as good as being dead. When it became known that I had been arrested by the State Research agents, everybody understandably gave up any hope of seeing me alive again.

On the morning of Friday, 9 September 1977, I was arrested by Amin's men at Entebbe International Airport. The morning had been fine and sunny, I went to the office early because I had no need to take the children to school during the school holidays. I'd finished all my travel arrangements and everything seemed to be going according to schedule. One reason I went to the office early was to leave some personal letters for my secretary to post, one to my wife and another to my mother, to advise them I was leaving for Montreal for an international meeting, the Assembly of the International Civil Aviation Organization which I was attending in my capacity as Director of Uganda's Civil Aviation Department. The directive for me to attend in person had come unexpectedly, leaving me no time to inform my family, who were in the countryside, working on our farm. I was to be absent for six weeks.

Just as I was about to leave my office, a friend dropped in. He was working on our farm project and needed transport. I promised to send him my driver as soon as I reached the airport, which was the first serious mistake I made in unknowingly isolating myself.

2

HOW THEY ARRESTED ME

Entebbe Airport is about thirty-five kilometres from the Ugandan capital, Kampala, where I had my office. It took half an hour to reach the airport and I released the driver immediately. As I was a bit early for the flight, I spent some time chatting with a friend of mine, Erison Musamya Kalibbala, who was on duty in the airport's briefing office. When the flight arrived, I left for the check-in counter and told Kalibbala not to wait for me but to go back to his office. This was another near-fatal mistake.

'Why should I go?' Kalibbala asked. 'There's no work and, after all, you're not even sure you'll go.' His doubt was based on the large number of passengers normally prevented from departing by the State Research boys.

'It doesn't matter,' I said. 'If I don't go, I'll give you a ring. In any case, I'll call the control tower to give me transport home.'

Kalibbala was reluctant to leave and we chatted for several minutes more. Then he said, 'This is a difficult period when everybody lives for the moment. A lot of people are disappearing daily, yet we don't know when this will end. How about our friend, Mr Kabanda? His body's still missing.'

Mr Kabanda had been the Commandant of Entebbe International Airport. He had been waylaid just a kilometre from the airport a few months earlier and his whereabouts were unknown. He had worked late that particular day over important information required urgently at his ministry's headquarters. After he and his accountant had finished, they had a drink at the airport bar before starting for home. Hardly out of the airport, they came upon a group of young men supposedly changing the back wheel of their car and stopped to lend a hand. The group were the State Research boys who had been waiting for them. Kabanda and his accountant were abducted and never seen again. Much later, I learned that Kabanda had been taken straight to Nakasero State Research Headquarters and locked up in the same cell I eventually occupied, before he was executed. His colleague's fate is unknown but he, too, was taken to Nakasero, although locked in a different cell.

We discussed this and the fruitless efforts which had been made to find Kabanda's body and then Kalibbala said, 'Wycliffe, you've led the department at a most difficult time. I don't envy you, but I wish you well.' With that he left.

The procedure at that time for all departing passengers was that when checking in, tickets had to be endorsed by a State Research official on duty. This officer was usually at a different counter, some twenty metres distant from the Sabena check-in. I was now joined by Louis Kerujik, an under-secretary in the ministry, who would be travelling with me to Montreal. Our delegation consisted of Lieutenant-Colonel Marijan, the minister leading us, Mr Ndaula from the Ministry of Justice, a Uganda Airlines official, ourselves and two State Research officials. It was a requirement at the time that all delegations include at least one State Research official.

In charge of the counter was a beautiful young woman (typical of Amin's agents at that time). She looked like a Rwandese girl or perhaps came from the Western Region of Uganda. She regarded us searchingly, then asked for our clearance to leave the country.

Nobody could leave Uganda without government permission. Initially this clearance was given by permanent secretaries and district commissioners, but subsequently the president was advised that entirely too many people were being cleared and decided to take on this job personally. Predictably, this soon proved unworkable because the president was too busy to sign all the required clearances. He then delegated this duty to his vice-

8

president, the Hon. Mustafa Adirisi, who found it a bother because, being almost illiterate, he could barely sign his name and it took him several minutes to affix a signature to each clearance. Therefore the clearance procedure was soon passed back to ministers.

Kerujik and I had been given clearance to leave the country by our minister, the Hon. Paul Etiang. It was this clearance that was being queried by the State Research girl and finally both of us ended up in the State Research office, on the left-hand side of the lounge as one entered the building. Inside the office, there was a lone woman sat in front of radio-communication equipment. She appeared fairly senior, in her mid-thirties, tall, with the I-II tribal marks on her cheeks, and she looked either Kakwa or Nubian. She wore a long dress, her eyes were red and she looked at us piercingly as if to see into our hearts. Serious and fierce, she showed us to seats but apparently did not know why we were there. We sat facing her, innocently waiting to have our clearance confirmed as genuine so that we could catch the Sabena flight due to depart soon. Although the wait was short it seemed like days.

Knowing the activities of the State Research boys, we wondered what might happen to us. I looked at the door, then at the woman, but neither offered me freedom. Young boys entered and went into the inner office, a few making remarks to the woman but none concerned with our presence. In the inner office, they appeared to be holding a meeting, and one of them kept peeping through to where we were and talking to the woman who still looked unconcerned. Finally they all left the office except one, who sat with his back to the inner office and faced all three of us. Short and slender, he was unlike his friends in that he had a light complexion which was a bit unusual for Kakwas and Nubians. He spoke in Nubian. Finally he walked out leaving us with the woman, but returned after some time to talk to her.

She asked my friend to give her his passport and, after reading almost every page of it, gave it back to him. Then another of the young men who had been at the inner-office meeting came and asked my friend to follow him out. That was the last time I ever saw Kerujik, but I learned later that he was permitted to leave,

9

caught the flight and made it to Montreal. I've never found evidence to support my suspicion that he was allowed to go free because he came from Amin's home area of Arua.

I remained alone, facing the State Research woman, my heart beating even harder as I was certain I was marked for death. I tried to calculate who would want me killed and why, and had no answers. I tried to convince myself I had a chance to stay alive because I was totally innocent of any possible misdemeanour.

I remained in that office about half an hour while the boys, about six in all, came in and out. During that time I thought of running away, I even prepared to do so, but when I stood up the woman also stood up and reached for a pistol on a nearby shelf. This significant move was an indication I might die before even reaching safety. I decided to sit tight and take no chances.

'Who are you?' the woman asked abruptly.

'I'm the Director of Civil Aviation,' I replied.

'Where do you come from?'

I presumed she wanted to know my tribe so I replied accordingly, but that didn't satisfy her and she made several telephone calls. She spoke in either Kakwa or Nubian, and although I couldn't understand her I was sure she was speaking about me.

My mind began to wander. I scolded myself for having sent away my driver and my friend, as they could have reported my disappearance. At the same time, I concluded that unless these boys killed me immediately and threw my body into Lake Victoria or into a forest or into the River Nile, I still had some remote chance of survival because I was confident I was innocent.

There were endless reasons for attracting the State Research boys, such as having a beautiful girlfriend, or wife or daughter. Strictness in the office could mean losing your life; ordering even office messengers about could spell danger, as could refusing to do a favour for a State Research boy. In Uganda, at the time, extreme care and caution had to be taken in even minor matters because, for example, even asking an office messenger to prepare tea could be interpreted as 'looking down' on him. The matter would be graver still if the messenger happened to belong to the 'royal' group. Being rich and prosperous was tantamount to a

10

death sentence. All State Research boys had a licence to kill so long as an excuse – any excuse no matter how flimsy – could be found. The system was to 'act on receipt of any report without making any investigation'. This meant that as soon as a report was received, a team was dispatched to kill whomever was reported on.

Not surprisingly, people were killed out of malice, revenge, envy or jealousy. Nevertheless, I still saw no reason for my arrest and thought that if I were not killed immediately and if, by lucky chance, some investigation were made, I would be found innocent. I had never patronized public bars nor associated with girls, so any conflict with the State Research boys because of girlfriends or liquor was out. I had never embezzled public funds nor ordered my juniors to do anything out of the ordinary.

After a while one of the boys returned and, arrogantly strolling into the office, said, 'Mzee' (a respectful Swahili word for 'old man'), 'as you said the minister is going on Monday, you too will go then.'

This further raised my hopes of being set free.

'Fine,' I said. 'In that case, let me have my passport so that I can go back home.'

'Well . . .' he drawled, as if he were about to add something he didn't quite know how to say, 'you may go home. But there is something we would like to discuss with you.' He spoke in very good Luganda; having realized I was a Muganda, he apparently wished to pretend friendliness by speaking to me reassuringly.

'OK,' I said, with more courage now that I had an indication as to why I was being held – and to me discussion really meant discussion and not a euphemism for something else. 'Please go ahead.'

'Not here, please,' he answered quickly. 'It's better we discuss outside. Come with me, here's your passport. Bring your brief-case. Where's your suitcase?'

I told him I didn't have one as I intended to buy one in Montreal as well as do some shopping there. His comments had shattered all my hopes of freedom, I realized I was under arrest, which usually equated with imminent liquidation. My heart galloped and I shook with sheer fright. I had no alternative but to stand up and follow him outside, but before reaching the door, I saw the woman press a button which was probably an intercom. The boy stopped and the one who had been sitting at the desk came in. After an exchange in Nubian, the woman passed a radio message to someone else. Then we left the room and entered the lounge.

I looked around frantically, searching for a face I knew with the intention of giving a signal that I was being kidnapped, but I saw no one familiar. I was discreetly led to a small yellow Japanese car, a Subaru, registration number UYK 745. I cursed myself again for having sent away both my driver and my friend. That was the first lesson I learned: there must always be someone to report whether or not one has actually caught a flight because while I was being led away to almost certain death, my friends, colleagues and relatives were sure I had gone to Montreal for six weeks. My disappearance would not be noticed for another two months.

Captain Raphael was the State Research officer in charge of airport operations. He had more power than ministers, because on a number of occasions he ordered the disappearance of VIPs waiting in the VIP lounge. I knew this man, having met him several times. On a few occasions I had also had some official dealings with him. Before we left the lounge I gambled that he could be of some assistance to me and asked if I could see him, but I was told that he was in the State House where we were going.

This remark heartened me a bit as only recently my officer in charge of air navigation services at Entebbe International Airport had been taken to the State House for interrogation and had come out alive. The ministry had asked me to look after some officials from the International Air Transport Association (IATA) who were visiting Uganda on a fact-finding mission because of the general deterioration of aviation services. After meetings in my office, we had visited the airport but, before going around, we had made certain we had permission to do so from the airport's military authorities. In fact, Lieutenant-Colonel Orombi, who

12

was in charge of aircraft operations, had accompanied us. He was picked up the following day and taken to the State House where he was interrogated about 'the team of white men he had taken around'. The interrogation was conducted in pitch darkness with physical torture included. The fear was that these IATA officials, being white, might have been connected with the Israelis who had raided the airport and rescued Amin's hostages about a year earlier. After this interrogation he was told: 'Next time you should be more careful taking foreigners around the airport.' Therefore when I learned I was being taken to the State House I hoped my interrogation might be similar, in which case I would come out alive.

We were seven in the car. The driver started off towards the State House but drove past the turn-off and on towards Kampala. Hundreds of ideas raced through my mind as I had no idea of our destination. I thought perhaps our 'discussions' were to be held in one of Kampala's state lodges. The boys were happy and talking merrily. They addressed me respectfully.

'*Mzee*, why are you so quiet?' one of them asked.

'I'm all right,' I said.

'If you're all right,' another said, 'then why do you keep quiet? Don't worry. Nothing will happen to you. It's only the big man who wants to have a word with you. Cheer up.'

Although I said I was all right, I was actually half dead with apprehension. Every time we approached a junction, I fully expected the car to turn off towards either a forest or Lake Victoria.

After that short conversation they continued to talk among themselves in both Nubian and Swahili. Fortunately, I had grown up with some Nubians and my long stay in Kenya and Tanzania had made me fluent in Swahili, so that I could pick up a few words from their talk. I heard the man who had been sitting at the desk in the office say, 'If he refuses, we'll take him to Jjajja Muwanga.'

Jjajja Muwanga was a slang expression I had picked up in Makindye prison, where I had been detained for a few weeks about nine months earlier. I had been transferred from Kenya to

13

Uganda and was staying with my family at the Imperial Hotel. I was still driving my car with a Kenyan registration plate. As Kenya was hostile to Amin, everything related to Kenya was suspect and I was arrested because of that Kenyan registration. Minister Marijan intervened and explained that I had been recently transferred, whereupon I was released. Jjajja Muwanga meant extreme torture. I deduced that if I didn't admit to whatever they wanted me to admit to, they would force a confession out of me. I recognized that torture was acceptable to me compared with immediate death, so much do our values alter in crisis. Again I dared hope, but all hope vanished when I saw my captors had pistols tucked in their socks. I was helpless. I began to pray silently for God's mercy, closing my eyes and trying to recite the Lord's Prayer, but I couldn't even remember its opening words. I was convinced even God had forsaken me.

These boys were amused to see me closing my eyes and burst out laughing. '*Totya* [don't be afraid], *Mzee*,' one of them said, 'you'll be all right.'

On entering Kampala, I was struck by what I saw at the Clock Tower roundabout, on the Katwe (south-western) side. Preparations were in progress for a firing squad which was due in a few hours. Empty drums were being wrapped in red cloth and were arranged in pairs, one atop the other. Nearby tree trunks were also wrapped in red; the soldiers wore red. All this indicated danger and I knew I was headed for danger, too. We drove past and I was briefly relieved.

From the Entebbe Road, we joined the Kampala Road, turned left up the Speke Road, past the Imperial Hotel where I had been picked up by the same fellows nine months before and continued on to the All Saints' Cathedral junction. This is the infamous junction where Amin claimed that the late Archbishop J. Luwum together with Ministers Oryema and Oboth-Ofumbi had died in a car accident. Almost past the cathedral, but on the right-hand side, we turned off into an enclosure.

We stopped briefly before being admitted. Noting the fence, I concluded this was the notorious Nakasero slaughterhouse. I admit I felt a measure of relief in being taken there as I hoped I

14

had at least a chance of survival after the 'investigation', having escaped immediate death.

It's hard to imagine that someone like me, who had already suffered several nasty experiences at the hands of the State Research boys and who knew I was almost certainly heading for death, still did not give up hope. It was only a few months since we had had to search through piles of dead bodies thrown into the well-known Namanve Forest for the body of my brother-in-law. That had been a bad experience. We had had to approach the area secretly. The local sub-chief had been bribed to lead us to the site but had cautioned us not to stay long because, should any soldier find us there, he would be shot. The spectacle of the dead bodies was unbearable. A few were fresh but most had rotted beyond recognition. Some had had their wrists cut off, possibly for the removal of watches. There was only one which had a watch and, surprisingly, it was still ticking. The sub-chief, as if to prove that Ugandans had become immune to such sights, grabbed the arm, chopped off the hand, removed the watch and put it in his pocket saying, 'This is my lucky day.'

We had then rolled the bodies over one by one, but failed to find that of my brother-in-law. On hearing a motor car, the sub-chief had ordered us to leave immediately, but asked for more money as we had exceeded the time period agreed upon for spending at the site.

I began arguing with myself. I'd come out of Makindye prison, so why not this one as well? I might be saved again as long as I could not be proved guilty of anything.

SKETCH PLAN OF AREA SURROUNDING NAKASERO STATE RESEARCH CENTRE

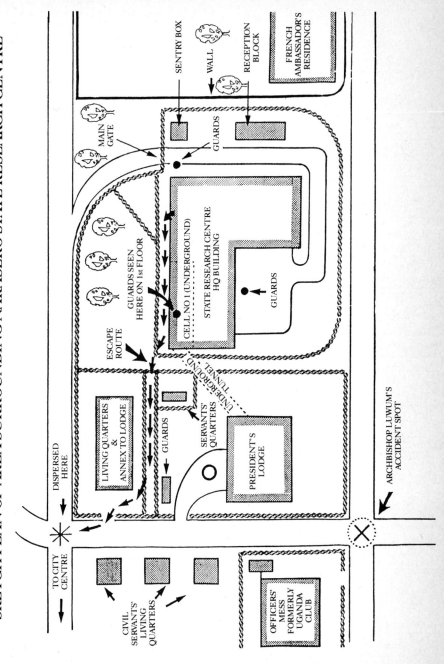

SKETCH PLAN OF NAKASERO UNDERGROUND CELLS

ESCAPE VENTILATOR

NARROW STAIRCASE
LEADING UPSTAIRS

TUNNEL BLOCKED
OFF HERE

CELL NO 1
PREVIOUSLY TUNNEL
LEADING TO
PRESIDENT'S LODGE

5 ft

CELL NO 2
PREVIOUSLY ARMOURY
FOR OBOTE'S
GENERAL SERVICE UNIT

IRON GATES

WOODEN TABLE FOR
SERVING FOOD

BUCKET FOR TOILET

PRISONERS' PROPERTY
DUMPED HERE
(IF NOT WORTH LOOTING)

TO PRESIDENT'S
LODGE

Prisoners' maps of the cells are, of course, identical as all the inmates knew every inch intimately. Major Kimumwe, killed in the liberation war of Uganda in 1979, together with two other of the Nakasero escapees, made this sketch. It was reproduced by the Kenyan monthly publication *Drum*, which also ran articles by him which fully corroborate the author's story.

PART TWO

LIVING IN HELL

3

NAKASERO AND THE OLD LADY

Nakasero State Research Headquarters was an L-shaped three-storey building and the reception area was on the ground floor where the two legs met. Nobody was at the reception table and there was no other furniture except a telephone on the floor. I was taken immediately to a cell on the ground floor, straight down the left-hand leg. The sole occupant was an old woman with swollen eyes and cheeks and a bruised face. She looked miserable and terribly worried. She wore a Ugandan long dress and sat on the floor at the far end, watching the boys treat me as chickens treat a stranger.

After escorting me into the cell the boys left me but returned almost at once with totally changed faces and aggressive manner, the very opposite of what they had been pretending to be like hitherto. Until then I had been addressed as '*Mzee*', but now they ordered peremptorily, 'Open up your briefcase, you stupid old fool.'

This was an indication of what was in store for me.

'Open up!' was what I heard from another but because they were slapping me I couldn't catch what followed. I was beaten up and kicked. My briefcase was thoroughly searched. They read all the papers in it, including a letter I was taking to a friend and former colleague working for the United Nations. This was used as an excuse for further beatings and I was accused of collaborating with the guerrillas. According to Amin, all Ugandans

21

outside Uganda were guerrillas. Another reason for the beatings was the Uganda Airlines ticket I had used a few days earlier. This, plus the letter, added up to my being a guerrilla although I had Adirisi, the vice-president's, signature on my clearance. I tried to explain how I had obtained that clearance but they paid no attention to me. They found nothing illegal or even suspicious on me or in my briefcase.

After the search, they left the cell. It was about two in the afternoon and I was left with the old woman, both of us silent until she asked, 'What's wrong, my dear son?'

'Nothing,' I answered.

'But then, why have they brought you here and beaten you up?'

I explained to her how I had come from the airport in the car with them, whereupon she asked, 'Then why did they arrest you if the vice-president himself had cleared you to go? Is it because of a motor car?'

'Maybe they thought I was trying to run away, but I wish they would advise my minister so that he could confirm I was going on official duties,' I replied.

With this we started a long conversation. First of all she advised me to pull myself together and be brave, because what I was to expect was worse than what I had already been through. Then she told me to put my things back in the briefcase. I squatted down on an empty Pepsi-Cola crate. She told me how people were tortured here, how women were raped and others killed. Although this was distressing, she encouraged me by saying that some torturing was just designed to obtain admissions of guilt and not intended to be fatal. The previous night she had been locked up with a married couple. Almost all the soldiers on the night shift had raped the wife, some of the raping done in front of the husband. I asked the old lady why she had been arrested and what had happened to her.

She told me how she was sitting outside her house one late afternoon when three youngsters from thirteen to fifteen years old approached her. After the usual long Ugandan greeting, one of them had asked, 'Would you like a blanket, madam?'

'No, thank you, my sons,' she answered. 'I'm not interested in blankets and I have no money.'

'Why aren't you interested?' the youngest asked. 'Don't you feel cold at night? Don't mind about cash, we don't want money. All we want is to save you from the cold weather.'

The lady declined but the boys pestered her until they became so abusive and aggressive that she gave in.

'You are a silly old woman! You must be stupid, too. Why don't you like the free gift of a blanket? You stupid old creatures die of the cold weather because you can't think of yourselves. You don't even know the usefulness of a blanket in this cold weather!' the eldest boy said.

After some long consideration the old lady accepted the blanket and gave the boys in exchange a big tin of coffee berries which she had brought from underneath her bed. This made the boys happy and they quickly left. The old lady was pleased, too, with her blanket, so much so that she spread it straightaway on her bed.

Unfortunately for all of them, the boys were arrested by the police at the railway station while waiting for a train. After a few slaps, they led the police to the old lady's home. It was about seven o'clock and getting dark. The old lady had entered her house and had lit her small paraffin light, known as *tadooba*. When she heard voices outside, she peeped out to see who was there and found two huge policemen standing in her doorway.

'Come out,' one of them ordered while the other pulled her outside by the neck. 'Where is the blanket?'

'Which one, sirs?' she asked, her voice trembling. 'Which one, sirs?' she repeated. Then she knelt like a typical Muganda asking for mercy. This, however, only proved the best position for receiving slaps and kicks. When she looked around and saw the three boys, she realized the gravity of her situation.

It was coffee-smuggling. Amin had issued several decrees aimed at reducing coffee-smuggling but, in spite of them, including one making it punishable by summary death, Ugandans continued to engage in this business because it was the best paid and the quickest. Better still, the money earned was in foreign currency. A good deal of coffee was being smuggled across the border to neighbouring countries, particularly Kenya and Rwanda. The business was best across Lake Victoria into Kenya and, consequently, Amin had established an anti-smuggling security force operating on the lake both day and night. Arrested coffee smugglers were dealt with by three people: Major Bob Astles (Amin's official adviser on British affairs), the Hon. Mustafa Adirisi and Amin himself. It was legal to shoot coffee smugglers on sight. The old woman knew this as did everybody else, and would know she was now in danger of being shot.

One of the policemen entered the house and brought out the blanket. The old woman was taken to Nakifuma police station where she was again beaten up. She remained there only a few days before she, together with the boys, was brought to the Nakasero slaughterhouse.

'My dear son,' she said and began to sob. 'My dear son, I must say I am worried because I am going to die. I am going to be killed like those people who were killed last night. Poor people, they were all innocent. My main worry is that none of my friends or relatives know where I am. Had my relatives known, I'm sure they would have bribed some top military officers to release me.' She wept piteously. 'Please do me a favour. Please help me. If you are lucky enough to leave this place alive, advise my daughter living in Najanankumbi [a suburb of Kampala] that I am here. I'm sure she will assist me. She used to have a major as her boyfriend a few years ago.'

She thought I might be one of the lucky few to be released from the hands of the State Research boys alive because I'd told her I was expecting my minister to help me out. Actually, this was expecting too much of anyone, ministers included. People did not, could not bail out or even appear to follow anybody kidnapped, or they'd be kidnapped themselves. I had the absurd but human hope that because I was innocent I might somehow get out of Nakasero alive. It might take a long time, but that was all right with me. Her conviction that I could and would call on her daughter added to my hope.

24

I had to take precautions, too. I gave her a similar message for my wife who, by coincidence, had the same name and was staying in the same suburb. We both undertook to advise each other's relatives if . . .

It was about 4 p.m. when food was brought to the woman. Nothing was given to me. It rained, and the fresh smell of the wet dust made the air taste sweet. We could see soldiers outside. Cars entered and left the enclosure. Soon the sun set, lights were switched on and my heart began to beat faster because of what I'd heard took place here at night.

About 8.30 p.m. three men came into the cell. Two of them I'd seen at the airport, the other was new. The new one beat me up without troubling to ask what wrong I had done. This was common, even routine in Amin's prisons. It was customary for soldiers to beat up prisoners without any reason or provocation. Fortunately one of the other two was sufficiently senior to have some sense of justice. He asked his colleague to stop beating me until he found out about my case. The man beating me stopped and I was hopeful some investigation would be made.

4

CELL 5

I was instructed to remove my shoes and socks, then led to another cell on the first floor. This was called Cell 5. Like the one below, it had formerly been an ordinary room with conventional glass windows. A beautiful girl was led out of Cell 5 into Cell 6. The two cells faced each other. She wore a brown skirt and white blouse and had no shoes.

From Cell 5 I could see the gate-keeper sentries as well as cars coming in and going out. I was handcuffed before being locked in the cell. This was a difficult moment because I lost what little hope had sustained me, and in spite of myself tears oozed from my tightly-shut eyelids. When I compared this situation with the one I had known in Makindye prison nine months before, I understood only too well that death was only a matter of minutes away. In Makindye we were locked up but not handcuffed.

The cell was large. I remembered the old woman's advice to die like a man so I pulled myself together and sat on the floor. This was the first time in my life I had been handcuffed. I wondered how I'd be able to stand up, scratch myself, eat – even practising a few of these actions – then I finally stood up and went to the window to look out. This was risky because I could easily have been shot from down below on the flimsy pretext of attempting to escape.

After some time I sat down and stretched out my legs.

I thought about my new briefcase, my wrist-watch and the

wedding ring the soldiers had taken from me. I lay down, tired, but found it very difficult as there was nothing at all on the floor and the handcuffs made it impossible for me to fold my hands. I lay with both hands stretched out above my head and rolled from side to side until I fell asleep from sheer exhaustion.

Around midnight I was awakened by noises. A man was begging for mercy and I heard the sounds of slaps and kicks followed by a sound of strangling. Then there was thumping, like the sound of a log of wood being booted about. This seemed to be the climax. I think it was a dead body being thrown on to a motor vehicle. I heard more cries. There was the sound of a machine, very much like a generator, being switched on. A woman screamed at the top of her lungs, but the screams turned into hums and oohs suggesting her mouth had been gagged. After a gunshot, there was the thumping again and that was apparently the end of the woman.

The next victim sounded like a Somali woman from her accent and was being questioned in Swahili. She was accused of spying; she was beaten up but I don't think she was killed. After a pause, a few gunshots sounded and then two people suspected of spying for Kenya were brought on the scene. From what I could overhear, these men had been picked up at the Speke Hotel and brought to this place. Despite the torture, the men insisted they were in Uganda on private business and that they had all the documents necessary to prove they had entered the country legally. After some silence, steps approached and I heard knocks on my cell door.

I froze, knowing it was a summons for me. The knocks grew louder; whoever was outside tried to open the door and even called out for someone inside to open. The door had been locked from outside and the light switched off from outside as well. After about ten minutes I heard steps receding and descending. I wasn't sure whether the intent had been to collect me or to rape the girl who had been in the cell before me. I was thoroughly frightened and lay down again on the floor rolling from side to side.

The following day was Saturday. I woke early and stood at the window, prudently hiding myself at one side. People moved in and out of the enclosure. I watched some birds flying and like all prisoners everywhere wished that I could fly, too. When I saw some butterflies, I envied them because they had the freedom I was being denied. I stared particularly in the direction of the city centre, past All Saints' Cathedral, hoping that by some marvellous chance the minister knew what had happened to me and had sent an appeal to the president, who, in turn, was sending someone to release me. All this turned out to be wishful thinking.

I heard more familiar and less threatening sounds, and realized the office workers had started their day. The noise increased and there were constant footsteps in the building. Around 9 a.m. I felt like going to the toilet, but there were no toilet facilities in the cell. I stood it for an hour or so, and then shouted for someone to come and take me to the toilet but there was no reply. I shouted harder, in vain. I shouted in English, Luganda and Swahili, shouting more in Swahili as most people in the State Research Bureau did not speak English.

Suddenly I heard a female voice respond to my appeals. I explained I wanted to go to the toilet. She asked whether I wanted to go for a long call.

'No – yes, madam. I want both calls but I am bursting,' I said.

'The officer who keeps the keys comes late, so you'll have to manage for some time,' she said.

'But I'm about to burst! Please ask the big officers to help me,' I asked desperately.

'If that's the case, I can only give you some advice.'

She told me to reach up to the shelf for an empty beer bottle and advised me to urinate into the bottle and empty it through the window. She cautioned me not to spill urine in the cell as that would put me in danger. I did as she advised, but it was difficult to accomplish. First of all I wanted to go for a long call, so I had to make sure I relieved myself of some pressure very carefully by passing out urine at intervals. Secondly, the bottle mouth being small, I found urinating straight into the bottle without spilling a problem. Then there was the matter of capacity. I had to repeat

28

the exercise several times before the pressure was reduced to an acceptable level. There was also the risk of pouring the urine over someone below the window. However, I suceeded, spilling only a drop of urine which I mopped up with my jacket.

Feeling normal again, I realized it was the girl in Cell 6 who had helped me, who knew about the bottle as she'd been locked in here before me. I smiled at her kindness and pitied her, because I could not imagine how she had managed the same exercise.

5

CELL 2, FINAL DESTINATION – LOCKED IN FOR GOOD

Around 2.30 p.m. footsteps came to my cell door, keys rattled and the door was opened. My shoes were returned to me and I was ordered to put them on and come out of the cell. I was puzzled, although the sight of another human being in the room pleased me. I thought the minister had sent a message to release me but the rough face of the soldier and the tone of his orders belied this. Had the intention been to free me, the handcuffs would have been removed.

Although I was pushed out and down the steps, I still cherished a faint hope of freedom, which was rudely dashed when I was told *'Chini, chini'* (meaning 'down down' in Swahili) at the reception. As we reached the bottom of the steps, I turned towards the entrance, assuming that I was being let out.

'Kwenda chini, we mjinga,' the soldier ordered in Swahili, meaning, 'Go down, you fool.' I continued down the steps. There were two flights of stairs to the basement and at the bottom was an area about ten metres by eight. We found thirty prisoners here, dying for lack of water. On the right was a small cell with a steel-bar gate and more prisoners. This cell was properly lit. On the left was another cell with a similar gate and, in addition, extensions of the gate on both sides, but these were not openable. I learned later that the cell on the right was Cell 1, and the other Cell 2. Unlike those in Cell 1, the prisoners in Cell 2 were

handcuffed. Those in the space between the cells were a mixture of both.

Rain had flowed through some ventilators into Cell 2 the previous night, and there was so much water that all the prisoners had spent the night standing. The prisoners were now using old sacks to dry the cell while the supervising soldier beat some with a big stick and kicked others. I was told to take the pail of water to empty outside under the escort of the soldier who had brought me.

When the whole area was dry, the prisoners were ordered to return to Cell 2. I'd already made a quick calculation and fervently wished I'd be assigned to Cell 1 where the prisoners weren't handcuffed. I was pushed into Cell 2 and ordered to leave my shoes in one of the large open cupboards. The soldiers locked up the cell and left. My shoes were later taken by another soldier who reported for night duty.

Cell 2 was fifteen by ten metres with a pillar in the centre. It had three long ventilators on the same side as the stairs, i.e. the back of the building. There were two big cupboards, a large table, much useless equipment and plenty of old cloth. In one corner, a big dustbin served as a toilet. There were now only seven occupants as fifteen had been taken and executed by a firing squad the day before.

6

MY CELLMATES

I expected the prisoners to be hostile to me but, to my surprise, they rushed and surrounded me asking me questions about what had happened outside in the three previous months while they had been imprisoned here.

The man who most impressed me was one-legged, his right leg having been amputated just below the knee. The stump was wrapped in a brownish bandage. He was talkative and hopped around with agility, without a walking stick. Another man was also outstanding — tall, broad-shouldered and with striking features.

'What happened to you?' the one-legged man asked.

'I don't know, but I suspect they thought I was trying to run away,' I replied and then told him my story. I asked them whether they had had lunch because, having missed the two previous meals, I was ravenous.

'What? A meal? We've not had lunch but don't worry, that's not the biggest problem,' the one-legged man said. The main problem was the constant fear of death, he said. Meals were irregular and, at one time, they spent four days without food. He encouraged me by saying that 'officially' we were supposed to be given regular meals, but the guards took the money allocated for meals for themselves instead of buying us food. In this respect I count myself lucky. The longest I remained without food was only two and a half days.

They asked me whether it was true their fifteen former cell-mates had been executed by a firing squad. They had been told of this firing squad during the tribunal hearings, but were not sure because the soldiers frequently played tricks on them, telling them that if they agreed to the wording of the soldiers' statements they would be set free. Several of the fifteen prisoners had signed statements of confession, incriminating themselves. The tribunal used these statements as propaganda, announcing to the entire world that the confessions were genuine and voluntarily made.

I told my new colleagues I had seen the firing-squad preparations and that I'd heard the sentries say that the shootings had taken place. The sentries chatted merrily about how the prisoners had been killed. 'It was a very good sight, one you'll never see again,' one had said. 'Most of them died after only a few shots, except that young man Nsereko. The boy must have been a magician, he just refused to die. The commander had to give fresh orders,' another had said. From their conversation I'd learned that some thirty-six bullets were fired into Nsereko's chest before he died.

After my confirmation there was silence. They realized their own fate was at best only hours away. At last, one said, 'We shall really die.'

'Let's die an honourable death,' another proposed, 'rather than by a firing squad.'

Supper was brought about seven o'clock, and I discovered how to eat with locked handcuffs. My new friends asked me several questions, trying to determine whether or not I was a spy, until they eventually concluded I was not.

I got to know them better as time went by. The one-legged man was Pilot Officer Cadet Nicodemus Kasujja Majwala from Bukolwa, Bulemezi County, in Buganda, aged twenty-seven. He was a helicopter pilot trained in the USSR. About five feet nine inches tall, he was not only the most vocal but also unbearably boastful. Everything about him was the best. He was the best pilot, although still a cadet, because he was Russian-trained. He was the best fighter, the strongest man and the most handsome.

His boastfulness often gave rise to heated arguments which sometimes came close to physical fights. For example, when we later had a serious diarrhoea outbreak because of food poisoning, Kasujja caused a great commotion when he claimed that he produced the least noise of any of us when on the dustbin.

He was a typical Mr Big Mouth and I suspect he had been among those responsible for giving away the plot in which he had been involved. It had been an obvious mistake to recruit such a person into the plan because in his need to claim credit for everything he was unable to keep a secret. It had been a plot to assassinate Amin and overthrow the government. Kasujja had been highly placed among the conspirators as he was deeply involved in recruiting participants. He also once drove a pick-up motor vehicle smuggling arms from the border into Kampala, a very courageous and daring assignment.

Kasujja had unquestionable courage. When he was shot in the leg on arrest, near Kisubi, he was taken to Amin in the Entebbe State House. Despite the imminent danger of death, Kasujja had told Amin, 'Please don't kill me. I'll direct you to where my friends are hiding.'

He then led the soldiers around the Kisubi area showing them the wrong places, pretending disbelief and consternation, while his friends fled the country. When the soldiers had had enough of this trickery, they took him back to Amin. 'Go and cut off his leg,' Amin had ordered the doctor he'd summoned from the hospital.

Kasujja was taken straight to the operating table where his right leg was amputated. The following afternoon, around three o'clock, a group of soldiers from Mbuya barracks came in an army Land Rover and demanded to take him away. 'Whom do you wish to see?' the nursing sister on duty had enquired. When they told her, sensing danger, she had called a doctor to explain how inadvisable it was to take a patient in Kasujja's condition from hospital. Both of them failed to make the soldiers see sense. They grabbed Kasujja off the bed and bundled him out of the ward and into their Land Rover.

The sister must have seen this act as tantamount to murder

because she'd cried out to them, 'Can't you behave like human beings?' She threw Kasujja a green gown, usually used in the operating theatre, and thrust medicine into his hand. He was taken straight to the Mbuya barracks where, after a day's interrogation, he was brought to the notorious Cell 2, then crammed with prisoners. The only clothing he had was his underpants and the green theatre gown.

Incredible things happened at Nakasero. In that climate and under those conditions, wounds turned septic if not properly treated, but Kasujja's leg miraculously healed with only the medicine the Entebbe Hospital nursing sister had given him, and the stitches were removed by one of his cell mates, Mutabazi. There was a time when, because of the pain, he had called out to the guards for assistance, but they were merely amused at his distress. 'Why don't you die and save us a bullet?' one of them advised.

Although Kasujja was a wise-acre he was also highly intelligent and creative. It was he who fashioned the cunning instrument which eased us of the torture of having to sleep with handcuffs on.

There was also Major Patrick Kimumwe from Kamuli, Northern Busoga, slender and fierce-looking and only thirty-one years old. At the time of his arrest, he was second-in-command of the Malire Mechanized Regiment at Bombo, and had been in the army for over twelve years. He was the most mature of the others, and probably because of this had been elected leader. He led us in prayers which we said at least three times daily. I came to know him better when I learned that we had been together at Busoga College, Mwiri, near Jinja, although he'd still been very young when I left.

Lieutenant Nambale was a small young man of about twenty-four, dark-skinned and easily irritated. He was born in Northern Bugishu. He trained as a jet pilot and, because of his aptitude and talent, he was made an instructor based at the Gulu Air Base. Undoubtedly this figured in his recruitment for the plot.

Lieutenant Silvester Mutumba was another young jet pilot from Busowa, in Southern Busoga. Also only twenty-four he was

35

the second-in-command of Amin's squadron of jet-fighter trainers with five and a half years' flying experience. The other three, though also from the Ugandan Air Force, were not pilots.

Warrant Officer II Christopher Ssekalo was dark-skinned with a powerful chest, but of only medium height. He was about thirty and came from Masaka in Southern Buganda. He was an airframes technician stationed at the Entebbe Air Force base. Although hot-tempered, he had considerable patience if left alone. This quality, together with his immense practicality, later proved invaluable to us. However, he was often put off or annoyed by Kasujja's boasting. He was good at playing draughts but often lost his temper when defeated – especially when Kasujja, laughing and bumptious, defeated him. At the same time he found Kasujja offered a good challenge because Kasujja was his equal. However, it wasn't unusual for their games to be abandoned because of disagreements.

Warrant Officer I Eddie Ssendawula was also from Masaka. Short, light-skinned and about thirty-three, he was mature and quiet, an aircraft airframes technician too. These technicians helped us a great deal in dismantling the film projectors that finally saved our lives.

Lastly, there was Warrant Officer II John Okech, from Buduma, near Tororo. He was about forty and also an airframes technician assigned to the Entebbe Air Force base. He was a tall, fat man with a broad chest, not as agile as his fellow military men, but strong, which later made him indispensable in our escape work. He was thoughtful and mature; there were many times when he used to let the others help themselves to food, even when we had waited days to be fed, before he took his share. His consideration and reasonableness contributed enormously to our survival.

7

GETTING TO KNOW EACH OTHER

It was relatively quiet that night except for minor incidents involving some guards who threatened to fight for possession of the personal belongings left in the cupboards in the open area between the two cells. It was customary for the soldiers to take all valuables from their victims. The apparent code for distribution was that the highest rank took the most valuable objects while the lowest had to be content with left-overs.

A smart young man was brought down by four soldiers, one of whom held a very expensive briefcase belonging to the victim. After he was locked up, in Cell 1, the soldiers started distributing the contents of the briefcase among themselves. The most senior, the sergeant, claimed the briefcase itself should belong to him because of his rank but the others refused, arguing he'd already received his share from the loot upstairs.

The smart young man had been found with about 150,000 shillings (approximately £1,500) and, because of this, was accused of '*intending* to buy coffee for smuggling'. When he was brought to Nakasero, the senior soldiers were so concerned about dividing his money that they forgot about the leather briefcase. The sergeant astutely brought it downstairs with the intention of appropriating it without the knowledge of his superiors who, under normal conditions, would have taken it. The acrimonious argument ended abruptly when the sergeant threatened to shoot his colleagues, pulling out his loaded pistol. As a poor substitute, more shoes were taken by the guards in the early hours.

When morning came, we prayed together, led by Major Kimumwe, and then we started what was to become our daily task of killing the lice in our clothes and hair and on our bodies. Then we gathered around the pillar to play draughts while making conversation. The conversation was more important to me than the game, because I came to know more about the place we were in, its surroundings and the fate awaiting us.

Nakasero was the main interrogation centre, and the execution room for Amin's State Research Bureau was on the ground floor. The flat three-storey building we were in is sandwiched between the president's lodge and the French ambassador's residence, about one kilometre from the centre of the city. Among us, only Major Kimumwe had any idea of the actual surroundings of the building because he had frequented the officers' mess, which wasn't far from the building. Facilities for holding prisoners were awkward and certainly primitive, probably because no prisoner was expected to survive, so what did it matter?

I was told how a tribunal had been conducted for the former cellmates and how they were finally led out to their death. Kasujja confirmed that killings went on simultaneously upstairs and in the cells below and showed me the bullet marks in our cell as proof. Cell 1 prisoners were made to carry out the bodies of those killed or found dead in the cells. One prisoner had been shot in the thigh by a guard who joked that he wanted to see someone cry in agony. He was left to bleed to death crying out 'Jogo, jogo . . .' meaning 'My lord, my lord, I am dying, please give me water to drink.' The guards laughed uproariously. The following morning his cellmates took the body upstairs.

The day of 8 September 1977 had been one of the worst in Nakasero. Prison arrangements had been stretched to the utmost with more than a hundred people in both cells; this included fifteen conspirators detained for their participation in Archbishop Luwum's alleged gun-running plot, plus a group of seven who had been involved in a genuine but abortive army/air force coup. They were packed liked sardines in the two cells and tempers were short, with fights resulting.

Okech, who with Ssendawula had first been locked up in Cell 1, said that Cell 1 had formerly been an emergency escape tunnel from the Nakasero Presidential Lodge to the outside. It was extremely hot because it had no air intake or outlet other than the gate leading upstairs. This was more of a transit detention hole for less important prisoners, such as robbers, murderers and coffee smugglers. The three youths who had been involved in the old lady's smuggling case were in this cell. Poor boys, they were constantly crying from sheer hunger. An old Kikuyu man from Kenya had been there for over six months. He had been arrested and locked up in the Naguru Police Barracks, formerly the most notorious execution centre. He had been attempting to smuggle a considerable amount of Kenyan money into the country and change it at a high rate. He was saved from there by a friend who bribed some of the top policemen. His escape was arranged, but he lost his way and he had to ask for directions from a good Samaritan who turned out to be a policeman in plain clothes. Instead of directing him to safety, this policeman escorted him to the Nakasero slaughterhouse, and he was locked up in Cell 1 without ever being formally charged. He had some money which he gave the guards in exchange for cigarettes. One day he asked a friendly guard for a razor blade with which to commit suicide. That was the day we heard a commotion in Cell 1. He had chewed and swallowed the razor blade. The guards were unconcerned. '*Wacha yeye akufe,*' meaning 'Let him die,' they said.

Kasujja then told us about his arrest and how several important people had been killed in our cell. The most recent had been Galabuzi Mukasa, a senior official in the Ministry of Culture. He had been alerted by his friends and urged to flee the country but, because he considered himself innocent, he decided not to do so. When he was picked up he was brought straight to this cell. We had a constant reminder of him because it was the wrist-watch that he had smuggled into the cell that helped us to know the time. When he was killed, his watch and his tweed jacket remained in the cell. Major Kimumwe decided to use the jacket.

Cell 2 was originally a windowless underground armoury for

the General Service Unit, according to Major Kimumwe. I asked him how the building came to be the headquarters of Amin's State Research Bureau. His explanation was that it had belonged to a similar organization in the previous regime.

Although physically our cell was better than Cell 1, operationally it was the more deadly. It was a dungeon for those 'condemned' to death. Only those people arrested on Amin's orders were locked up in this cell, and only three people could authorize our 'release' (i.e. death). These were Amin, Adrisi and Bob Astles. Apparently this saved us from some harassment by ordinary guards. If, by any chance, any of us got killed without Amin's knowledge, a report had to be sent to him. The longer we stayed in Cell 2 the more intimate we became.

'Actually, Mr Kato, we have no hope of surviving,' said Ssendawula. 'We've been here for about three months but we've never seen anyone released from here.'

'But if we're innocent,' I protested, 'surely their investigations will prove it.'

'Investigations! You must be joking. Not here,' said Kasujja.

'The best solution is to escape,' Ssendawula pronounced.

There was complete silence which suggested that his friends disapproved of the idea being discussed so early in our acquaintance. The topic was dropped and other matters considered until we heard descending footsteps and the jangle of keys. Two of the Entebbe Airport boys came to our gate and called out, 'Where is the Director of Civil Aviation?' Nobody replied. I had been cautioned about just such calls and was terrified.

'Where is the Director of Civil Aviation? Are you deaf, you fools?' The man who looked like the leader of the Entebbe group raised his voice to shout.

'Here I am, sir,' I said.

My mind went over several possibilities from immediate death to freedom. The two faces looked familiar. They could be here to take me to my place of execution, to see my minister or to see the president. Since I hadn't been told what I was charged with, I suspected it was something to do with my clearance for leaving the country. I wanted to think my minister had been advised that

I was here and that he had sent me the correct clearance. I therefore moved to the gate with hope in my heart.

'Yes, *Efendi*,' I said politely.

A sheaf of narrow papers was pushed at me. 'Sign all of them. Make sure you use your usual signature,' the leader told me and the second man added carelessly, 'If you don't, you'll die right now.'

I recognized the travellers' cheques I had been carrying for my trip. As I had no choice, I complied and returned the signed cheques to them. They went upstairs but returned within ten minutes, raging with fury. One was carrying my passport and the other the signed cheques. 'Look!' said the leader. 'Your signature on the cheques is different from that in your passport. Sign again! And this time sign on the back of each leaf as well.'

I did so and 3,600 dollars were taken from me.

'Don't worry,' Kasujja consoled me. 'Now that they've taken all that money you might be released. After all, they've no serious case against you. How I wish I were you!'

This made me feel better and I smiled a bit. Then I realized that I had little reason to be optimistic. 'But how could that be? You say nobody's ever been released from here. How could I be released? I'd be the first one!'

Nevertheless, deep within me, I hoped my money might save me.

After some time Nambale mumbled, 'You, Kasujja, are stupid. I'm sorry, but I've told you several times. Don't you think the money only brings his death closer? These soldiers will feel too guilty to release him. Their taking the money so openly only goes to show they don't expect any of us to come out of here alive.'

This comment dashed the little hope I'd gained. I had to admit it seemed to be the most logical conclusion. I was most likely going to be killed, and it would be two months before anyone would be alerted to my disappearance. We talked again about the innocent people who had already faced the firing squad. I understood that only three had confidentially admitted to having taken part in the plot. There were nine who appeared completely

41

innocent. This disturbed us considerably, as we knew we might be the next victims of the live target practice. Fortunately for me, my friends were by now convinced I was not a spy, and they told me about some important people who had lost their lives. As a result we gradually agreed there was but one course of action open to us. We must escape.

8

WE MUST ESCAPE
. . . BUT HOW?

Nobody had ever escaped from Nakasero, but in trying to we had nothing to lose. We knew we'd eventually be killed whether or not we attempted to escape, so the sensible thing was to work out a plan.

We knelt down and prayed to God to protect and guide us. Our main object would be to save our lives and, since we knew very well Amin would not forgive us if we were caught, we prayed, too, for understanding of whatever lengths we might be driven to. All of us knew tomorrow's firing squad, or one the day after, or soon, would be for us. It was important we act quickly.

We studied the situation. One suggestion was that we seize the key of the cell from the guard and, at an appropriate time, break out and fight our way past the rest of the guards. Another was that we try to make our own key. The first suggestion looked too risky, while the second appeared too difficult. We had no tools and the padlock was frequently changed.

We had a long and careful look at the four ventilators at the top of the wall. They opened out at ground level and each was about three feet long and one and a half feet high. They contained several thick iron bars embedded deep into the massive concrete walls. Behind the bars were two layers of hard wire gauze and behind the wire were slanting glass louvres.

'Gentlemen,' said Ssendawula, 'there is our saviour.'

'Where is He?' I asked excitedly.

'That one there.' He pointed to the ventilators which each of us was intently studying. There was a chance here. We remembered from our childhood experiences that whatever a head can go through the rest of the body can follow. If we could get rid of the gauze and glass and make a space to lever away at the bars, without being detected and before the deadline of the firing squad, we had a chance, however slim. We had a two-fold problem: we were handcuffed and we had no tools of any sort.

The hindrance of handcuffs was minimized because of Nicodemus Kasujja's intelligence and practicality. Although our cell was a mess and a mass of rubbish, this turned out to be providential as the jumble yielded pieces of metal, shoes, cloth and electric cables.

A few days before the previous executions, Kasujja had found a small piece of metal in the rubbish and had painstakingly ground it to a sharp point against the concrete floor. He had then used it to release the spring on his handcuffs until they opened. After that he opened other handcuffs, and eventually all Kasujja's friends were secretly freed. The 'secret' was quickly passed on to those in the Archbishop Luwum group who Kasujja felt could keep it even faced with the clear danger of an imminent firing squad. Sleeping on a bare floor is bad enough but doing so in handcuffs makes any sleep difficult and uncomfortable. From that time on, every night after lights went out, Kasujja opened the right-hand cuffs to make sleeping easier.

Things were slightly different for me because my handcuffs couldn't be opened by Kasujja's improvised tool. While my new friends were having relatively restful nights. I had to sleep in my handcuffs until one day I was lucky enough to be taken for a shower. Normally we were not permitted showers or baths except when we were taken to face senior soldiers for interrogation. No doubt the officers anticipated our high odour and gave instructions for us to be showered. This time, because we were due for special interrogation, we were taken to the first floor for our showers.

Earlier on, when trying to open my handcuffs, we had realized that my left one could be pulled off by force. I gave the guard my right hand and he opened the handcuff so I could shower properly: after the shower I asked Ssendawula to relock it loosely. When my turn came for locking, the guard merely thanked me for being a good prisoner who willingly locked his own hand-cuffs. From then on I, too, had easy nights.

Although Kasujja's boastfulness had been detestable, this time it was acceptable. By giving credit where credit was due, every-one was grateful to him and didn't mind how much and how often he spoke about it. Kasujja even made a duplicate tool to speed things up, as he put it, but actually as further proof of his intelligence which, combined with his Russian training, was far above ours – or so he insisted and we didn't contradict him.

Locking ourselves up again at first light was easy. My friends just snapped the ends of their cuffs together while I rolled mine back on. The cuffs were locked without needing a tool but because of the unavoidable clicking noise it was essential to lock them away from the gate when no guard was around.

None of our guards ever knew about, or even suspected, our achievement, probably because they were untrained as prison warders. As far as they were concerned we were potential corpses, not prisoners. This was a small but vital triumph we managed to keep entirely secret.

9

MY ARREST IS KNOWN

Going for a shower was a blessing for me in another way. When I came back I bumped into a soldier who'd been with me on an official trip to Lome, Togo, Lieutenant Sande Diobe. He was light-skinned, of medium size and height and far too talkative to be with, particularly in a foreign country where he'd tried to bully his way about as the State Research officials did in Uganda. He strongly resembled a Rwandese, but he called himself a Ugandan from Jinja. His academic qualifications were almost non-existent, which was embarrassing to his colleagues when he tried to show off.

Diobe and another State Research official called Peter had accompanied several of us to a meeting of the African Civil Aviation Commission. When he saw me in Nakasero only three months later and handcuffed, his astonishment was understandable.

'Mr Kato! What's happened to you?' he blurted.

I kept quiet because it was an offence for a prisoner to talk to anyone without the guard's express permission, but after he'd repeated his question three times I finally said I didn't know. Fortunately he followed me down to the cell some ten minutes later, again expressed surprise and after some conversation asked, 'What can I do for you?'

In the circumstances, this was just about the most difficult question to answer, and I'm certain he had no idea what such a

46

casual-seeming question meant to me. I wanted to ask him to have me released but feared to do so.

'Tell me how you want me to assist you,' he urged.

I couldn't let this opportunity slip by.

'Please go and let my office know I am here and not in Montreal,' I asked him. 'Let them advise the minister and my wife.' This was my first message from prison, and because of Lieutenant Diobe, my colleagues, friends and family learned what had happened to me.

Although Diobe didn't know my office, he knew Mr Wamae in the ministry headquarters in Amber House who had led our delegation to West Africa. Mr Wamae took him to my office and as a result Mr Mathias Kiganira Mukasa, a colleague and a close friend of mine, took up the issue of my arrest with the responsible authorities. He even approached high-ranking military officers, but in vain.

My wife fainted when Mr Mukasa brought her the bad news, my mother was deeply shocked and my children wept because they knew it was only a matter of time before I was killed. It was common knowledge that soldiers were tricking relatives of victims into believing the victim was still alive so that the soldiers could extort substantial sums of money as a form of ransom. Therefore my people doubted the genuineness of this verbal message from me, and asked Diobe to bring something in writing, signed by me.

About 8 p.m. the following day I saw Diobe again, in high spirits and talking with embarrassing, even dangerous loudness.

'Where's Mr Kato?' he was shouting.

'I'm here,' I replied softly.

'Your people doubted my word, so please write them a note.'

Of course I, in turn, doubted whether he'd actually been to see them. I asked him for a pen and paper and wrote a short note which he did, in fact, deliver.

10

STUDYING OUR WINDOWS

Having solved the problem of handcuffs, we tackled the others. The wire gauze was the first. It had been decided earlier that day that it would be best to try to escape during the night, but I had foolishly opted out. I was still debating the risks both ways and decided to chance staying in prison to await a possible investigation which I was convinced could be arranged for me. I also thoroughly disliked the idea of living alone as a refugee for the rest of *my* life because Amin had vowed to rule Uganda for the duration of *his* life. I told my friends, 'I'm sorry, but I've decided against escaping for the sake of my family.'

'Please, Mr Kato, think again. If you stay here, you'll be killed. That won't help your family,' Ssekalo said.

After thinking it over again I told them that, considering none of us knew what was outside and the high probability of being shot while climbing the prison fences, I was all for them going while I remained, but asked them to let me know when they planned to make their break.

We had underestimated the problem of cutting the wire and had misjudged the size of the gaps between the bars. Looking at the gaps from below they had seemed large enough for our heads but, in reality, they were not. With the wire gauze being far too strong to tear and the four-inch gaps between the bars too narrow for any head to go through, and the bars themselves firm as a rock, there was no alternative save to wait until the next night and try again.

They converged on me to insist I give up the idea of staying behind, repeating stories of innocent and important people who'd been killed here. After deep thought, I capitulated. I felt I'd received a message from God because finally I understood I had no other chance of survival. This pleased my friends. Before we made another start, we scrambled around among the rubbish until we had quite a treasury of old nails, spoons and other pieces of metal. What was needed was perseverance and patience, because the job was difficult and we were working against time. Fortunately Ssekalo volunteered to do the cutting this time, and he displayed the wealth of knowledge we were looking for. Slowly, terribly slowly, but effectively, he went on breaking the wire gauze, piece by piece, until he had forced a tiny way through to the slanting piece of glass.

At this point we experienced a moment of triumph, but it was quickly dashed when Sergeant Major Ssekalo found that the wooden frame of the glass louvres had been securely fixed into the cement and would not come out. He would have to break the glass. He stayed up there, puzzled, not knowing what to do. Finally he signalled he was coming down, which we interpreted to mean he'd heard someone outside and wanted to let him walk past our spot. Once he'd informed us of the obstacle, we agreed we had no option but to continue with the plan. He climbed up the wooden boxes again and carefully broke one glass louvre. The noise it made seemed to us so loud that for a long heart-stopping moment we awaited the arrival of Amin's thugs. We were lucky; apparently it had gone unnoticed and we continued our work with the greatest caution.

We had to devise some effective means of muffling the sound. Kasujja leapt enthusiastically into the breach, choosing this opportunity to lecture us on how silent Russian guns could be. He tried to prove his case by adding that the guns used by the Israelis in the Entebbe raid were of Russian make. None of us could take this seriously, and we burst out laughing.

'But you, Kasujja, must be very stupid,' Nambale said. 'How

do you expect us to believe that? Russians and Israelis don't see eye to eye. The Israelis would never buy ammunition from Russia, nor would the Russians sell it to them. And most important, the Israelis can make their own guns with silencers, after all they're known for making sophisticated equipment.'

'Let's excuse him because he thought the rescue of the hostages would make them friends,' Okech interposed.

'I'm not as stupid, nor as naive as you think,' Kasujja burst out, nettled. 'I know what I'm talking about. I know Israel is now a mini super-power, but it imports most of its technology from Jews in the United States and South Africa. What would stop Israel from doing likewise with Russian Jews? This is plain common sense which some of you seem to lack.'

'United States Jews are rich,' somebody interposed. 'Russian Jews aren't. They're not even allowed to practise Jewry.'

'These whites are the same,' Kasujja rushed on, unheeding, 'particularly when there's a crisis affecting them. After all, what's a black person to any white man? Which of those mighty world powers advocating human rights came to our rescue when Archbishop Luwum was murdered? You wise men would expect the USA or France or Belgium to send in commandos to kidnap Amin. But what happened? Nothing!'

'Mr Kasujja, listen,' said Major Kimumwe patiently, 'those are civilized countries. In the civilized world no state interferes in the internal affairs of another state.'

'Civilized countries!' Kasujja interrupted. 'What do you mean by "civilized countries"? You mean those selfish, greedy, rotten capitalists?'

'Of course he can't mean Russia,' Okech inserted with seeming innocence. 'He knows perfectly well what Russia does to small countries like Hungary when it dislikes their policies. Anyway, we're not talking about capitalism, communism or socialism. We just want a solution to our glass louvres. Let's not waste time.'

'No, John,' Major Kimumwe said quietly. 'Let me teach this kid who is mad about communism the bad things about it so that he can see the other side of the coin. Communism means slavery, suppression, exploitation by a class rather than an individual as in capitalism. It means elimination of opponents by force and often in secrecy, just to mention some of the evils of communism. Socialism is the offspring of communism. That is why we, enlightened people of Uganda, don't want to hear anything about them. For your information, the last president who tried to turn us into socialists ended up in Tanzania, a socialist state where everyone has to sing "socialism or Ujamaa".'

This statement further irritated Kasujja. He hopped about as he retorted: 'Even you, sir, are a big fool. Capitalists cheat you with baits that blind you. You implied capitalists don't use force. What did the Americans do in Vietnam? And wasn't it because of the gold and the minerals that the Belgians, together with their greedy capitalist allies, fought in the Belgian Congo which we now call Zaire? I'm sure if Uganda was very rich and tried to kick out any capitalist country or kill nationals of such a country, you'd see B52s swarming about our sky like kites on a hot day.'

'I don't think that's strictly correct, Mr Kasujja,' I said. 'We had Canadians monopolizing our copper industry in Kilembe. When Amin kicked them out for taking all the copper practically gratis, they just left.'

'Ah, but watch what they're doing,' Kasujja replied. 'They're just keeping an eye on events here. As soon as Amin is assassinated they'll be the first to come back and welcome the new government. This time, though, they'll come with even more tempting baits. You'll see.'

Footsteps disturbed us. Everyone squatted in his usual place. Guards were bringing someone new to Cell 1; they locked him in and left.

We re-examined our problem. Among all the other junk in the cell were the dirty sacks on which we slept and a collection of blood-stained, filthy old shirts and trousers previously owned by those the firing squad had killed, those killed in the cell or those slaughtered in the extermination room on the ground floor, directly above us. We urged Ssekalo to cover each piece of louvre with a bundle of the clothes before breaking it. This suppressed the sharpness of the noise, dulling it, just like firing a gun with a silencer. Slowly and with extreme care he succeeded in extracting

51

all the fragments of glass. Now he had to cut more of the wire gauze before we could have a go at the bars. We did not want to operate outside official working hours, so we had to postpone this until the following day.

Working at night involved too many risks. Noise travels far at night and we could never know who might be listening outside. We decided to post night-watches to ascertain what was happening outside. We established that the guards went around the back of the building – our proposed escape route – every even hour, which meant 1 a.m and 3 a.m were the hours most favourable for our plan. There was nothing else constructive we could do at night. We lay awake and thought of death, death and nothing but death. Death was coming nearer and nearer every hour. We knew we would die soon, unless God saved us through that ventilator. Sometimes one of us would summon up the resolution to say, 'Let us die like men,' but it was impossible to accept death. One has to fight until overcome by death itself.

The sentries often came down to check on us and to relieve their boredom by hurling streams of abuse at us in Kakwa, Lugbara and Nubian. They said this was their revenge for the old times when the northerners had always been the underdogs, the slaves of the southerners. It was their turn now as Amin, their saviour, had turned the tables. They goaded us, saying we were at their mercy and they could make us eat our own shit or theirs. They could shoot us at will and so on. We had heard so much similar abuse that we'd become immune to it. In fact, until a few weeks earlier guards had come freely to shoot prisoners as they pleased but apparently this liberty had been rescinded. Not everyone was allowed downstairs. We were not particularly worried; after all we were absorbed in our planned escape. Additionally, like most Ugandans, we were accustomed to the brutality and rudeness of Ugandan soldiers. It was as though the current Ugandan law entitled them to steal, rob, beat up and kill anyone they chose because there was nobody to complain to. They regarded the civil police as toothless bulls, and the courts were left to deal with cases not involving any Ugandan soldier or any of Amin's other special civilian people. It was only proper that we disregard their insults. With our heads full of escape plans it would have been foolish to cause any trouble that might lead to a search of our cell and so expedite our execution.

11

AN IMPOSSIBLE TASK

It took Ssekalo several days to finish cutting through the layers of wire gauze. When this was done, we were face to face with those immovable iron bars. We were so near to our goal and yet so distant.

Ssekalo was the first to be disappointed. He tried to fit his head through the gap only to find that his head was too big. When he tried wrenching at the bars there was no indication that any of them could be bent by sheer force. He came down, shaking his head. 'It's impossible,' he told us. 'There's just no chance. I'm afraid we are going to have to die here.'

Each of us wanted to prove to himself that the gap was too small for his head. One by one we climbed up and then, discouraged, came down. Not even the small head of Mutumba could fit through. We realized what an enormous ovestimation we'd made of that all-important gap. Even Kasujja, who claimed to have sufficient strength to pull the bars apart, was quiet. The obstacle appeared insurmountable.

'What do we do next?' Nambale asked.

'Let us pray,' answered Major Kimumwe and Okech together as if they had rehearsed it. We knelt and Kimumwe led us in our prayers. We had elected him our leader to ensure maximum discipline. He had been leading us in most of our prayers and, unlike the usual long ones, these were short and, surprisingly, only for the dead.

Aware of the magnitude of the task we faced, we further tightened our security. Whenever we did anything active, we posted someone at the gate and another one at the ventilators, neither of them allowed to remove his handcuffs. Their duty was to watch and listen for anyone coming.

One-legged Kasujja was obviously the most suitable for the gate position as, being naturally talkative, he could keep an inquisitive prisoner in Cell 1 occupied with the necessary jokes. Secondly, his disability proved him useless for the next stage of our work which required much exertion and considerable strength. Finally, being a smoker and a joker he was handy in chasing away all undesirable characters who came to our gate. The strategy was to ask anyone who approached the gate for a cigarette. This made us unpopular with the guards, so much so that everyone walked off hurriedly muttering insults and making our objective that much easier to achieve.

We took turns at the ventilator position. We had to listen for any outside sound, and also had to peer through the slanting glass louvres for any possible sign of movement. Our code words for Amin's thugs were 'rat' in English, Luganda (*messe*) and Swahili (*panya*). We deliberately selected these words because of the great number of rats that infested our cells. Mentioning 'rat' served two purposes: the first was to alert our friends and the second was intended for Kasujja at the gate to start a conversation on a worthwhile topic Amin's thugs could easily follow.

Our other precaution was to hide the hole we had made in the ventilator. Since we had removed a section of the multi-coloured louvres and the wire gauze, more light was now coming through. We'd purposely selected the ventilator in the left-hand corner nearest the gate because it was the most difficult to see from the gate, but even without the light, the hole was visible from the cell gate. We put up a small rail from which we hung a shirt so that it obscured the hole. Then we folded up a few sacks and put them in the ventilator. This looked quite normal because every morning we swept the cell and hung up any bedding.

We re-examined our working programme and since time was important to us, though not as important as not being heard, we confirmed our previous decision to work only during office hours. We started when the State Research staff arrived at work in the mornings and the general hubbub was sufficient to cover our scrabblings and rustlings.

While we were so deeply concerned about getting our heads through the all-too-small gap, Kasujja said, 'Why don't we shrink our heads as a solution?' We were too worried to respond to a joke. 'If I had been trained in China,' he continued, 'I would have been a magician and passing our heads through that gap wouldn't be the problem it now is.' Nobody responded.

Then something came to my mind. If we could relax the tension of our minds we could come up with new ideas in time. Meanwhile, I did not understand why Major Kimumwe had decided to pray only for the 'dead ones' whereas we normally asked God to give us the courage to go through with our plans and keep the guards both deaf and blind. I asked him. 'Why only for the dead?'

'Well,' he began slowly, 'I think even God has forgotten Ugandans. Can you imagine that even when Amin murdered his shepherd Archbishop Luwum in this prison, nobody came to save us? Now, look, I am sure that the Archbishop of Canterbury, the Queen of England and her ministers and the holy Pope in the Vatican all know how Archbishop Luwum was killed. Then why didn't God Almighty give them the courage to come forward and dispose of the murderer? Instead, apparently He's given Amin's thugs more power to kill even more innocent Ugandans.'

'But, Patrick,' I protested, 'we shouldn't despair. Maybe He will save us one day.'

'When will that day come? You mean God is waiting for all Ugandans to die so that He can send His only Son again to save us? I think it is high time we questioned ourselves as to whether God is still on our side.'

'But then why did you pray only for the dead?' I persisted.

'Actually, it was because we are as good as dead,' he explained. 'That's why I pray for the dead, to include ourselves in the dead so that our souls may rest in peace,'

'But, Major Kimumwe,' Okech objected, 'surely we should

pray for our souls to be taken to heaven like that of the Archbishop.'

Major Kimumwe seemed unconcerned about going to heaven. Meanwhile Ssekalo and Kasujja continued playing draughts. After some time I reminded my friends of the obstacle and asked the crucial question.

12

HOW SHALL WE
BEND THOSE BARS?

'Now gentlemen, how shall we bend those bars?'

'With those,' Ssendawula joked, pointing to the discarded film projectors in one corner of the cell.

I looked at them in silence. Kasujja and Ssekalo also looked; Kasujja began to giggle. At that moment we heard voices outside by the ventilators and we froze with fear. Our hole was sure to be seen at such close quarters. Someone was instructing unseen bricklayers to close off the ventilators to stop rainwater flowing through them into the cells as had happened a few days ago. There was no way the bricklayers could miss our hole, and, once again, death would be imminent. Ssendawula broke into our silent terror.

'Well, gentlemen, let's not be unduly worried because whether we worry or not, we shall die if God says so. Otherwise, if God has not given up, we shall not die.'

'That's true,' Major Kimumwe agreed, 'but when will He hear our prayers?'

'Anyway,' Ssendawula continued, 'let's use everything as the situation dictates, we have nothing to lose. Let's whisper to these workmen when they come and ask them to bring us a hack-saw so that we can cut these iron bars. I'm sure they'll be willing to assist their fellow Ugandans on the point of death. God may be helping us through them.'

'Yes, but suppose some of those workmen are State Research men?' Nambale asked. 'Won't we have sold ourselves?'

'It's true,' Okech admitted. 'But this is called "Hobson's choice". Either way, we'll die. We might as well select the way where there seems the chance of getting sympathy from fellow human beings.'

We agreed we should take the risk. Meanwhile our most pressing objective was to bend the bars enough to let us wriggle through to freedom, preferably before the bricklayers started work. We badly needed two things, a bending instrument and the energy to use it. Incredibly, in the accumulated debris in the cell were two cast-iron stands on which the old unserviceable Russian-made film projectors, also of cast iron, were mounted. Each projector stood on a metal column which was fixed to a base made of two diagonal metal pieces. Again, it was Ssendawula who drew our attention to them. 'Look here, gentlemen,' he said seriously, 'we can use these stands to bend the bars. What do you think?'

'That's a good suggestion,' I agreed. 'But how do we dismantle them? We have no tools at all, not even a screwdriver.'

Fortunately we had Ssendawula, Ssekalo and Okech who were all three trained mechanics. They volunteered to dismantle the projectors. We put on a show, pretending that Ssendawula was just idly looking at the projector while Ssekalo and Okech watched him in such a position as to obstruct anyone's view from outside the cell gate. Kasujja was, as usual, posted at the gate, alert to distract any possible enquiries or unwanted attention from the Cell 1 prisoners, someone else was at the ventilators and the rest of us played an innocent game of draughts. Everything went well until Kasujja shouted '*Messe!*' Each of us jumped to our pre-determined positions. This was a big 'rat'. A guard was coming down the stairs.

'*Efendi, nipatie sigara,*' Kasujja wheedled. 'My lord, please give me some cigarettes.'

The guard merely looked at him without interest and went back. Kasujja gave the thumbs-up signal to indicate that we could resume our clandestine work. It was fascinating to watch

Ssendawula. Using only his fingers at first he removed piece after piece and fashioned some in such a way that they could be used to dismantle the rest of the projector. It took him a full day to unscrew one stand.

One essential, energy, was hard to come by. Although we were supposedly fed daily, there were many days running when we had nothing at all to eat. When something was finally given us, it was cassava and potatoes from the well-known Shauri Yako market in the city. This market is notorious throughout Uganda, even to people who have never been to Kampala, for its filth and thieves. '*Shauri yako*' is Swahili for 'it's your own affair', and means that you buy anything from there at your own risk. No seller cares whether his merchandise is good or bad. When an unlucky thief is caught, instant judgement is administered by the market mob. Normally this means death on the spot.

The food we were brought usually included beans or a sauce made from the heads of cattle; this gave us diarrhoea. We rarely received drinking water, and when we did, it was invariably a quarter of a cupful each. It could be a day or two before someone remembered us. Hunger and thirst sometimes made us quarrel among ourselves, but we quickly realized the pointlessness of this and came together again.

On 13 September 1977 at about 2 p.m. we inserted the projector stand between the iron bars for the first time, using the diagonal base, because the head of the stand was too big to fit through the gap. Initially there was considerable undesirable noise from the metal rubbing against metal, but we eliminated this by rolling old shirts around the base before inserting it. The stand was now above our heads, so we had to climb on wooden boxes to reach it and lever it so that at least one bar bent. This was far from easy. We pushed, sweated and strained without any sign of success. At about 4.30 p.m., exhausted and discouraged, we decided to call it quits until the following morning.

At 9 a.m. we were at it again, but could still effect no change. Around 11 a.m. we heard Kasujja call out '*Panya!*' and we hastily pulled out the stand, hid it in the rubbish and took up our assigned positions. Kasujja said, urgently, '*Emesse!*' and looked in

60

our direction to confirm we'd understood the message because he saw someone coming down the steps approaching our gate.

'*Unasema nini?*' Amin's thug shouted. 'What are you saying?' Kasujja, in his excitement as he saw us still fumbling with the stand as the guard approached, had spoken loudly and the guard had heard him. '*Unasema nini, wewe mabusu?*' the guard shouted again, meaning, 'What are you saying, you prisoner?'

Cunning Kasujja replied, '*Efendi, kuna panya n–y–i–n–g–i hapa,*' or 'My lord, there are p–l–e–n–t–y of rats here.'

Amin's guard thought Kasujja was pointing out the rats which were actually scuttling among the plates which hadn't been collected from the previous day. '*Aya,*' he said, '*wacha hata panya wakule mabusu,*' which meant, 'All right, let the rats also feed on the prisoners.'

This thug had come down to look for any possible valuables belonging to the new prisoners which could have been left the night before. His presence was dangerous to us, so Kasujja was at him again. '*Efendi, nipatie sigara.*' He asked for cigarettes but the thug paid no attention to him. Kasujja hopped around the gate, pushed out his two hands and begged again. This annoyed the thug who turned and made as if to strike Kasujja, shouting, '*Kwa nini unaniuliza sigara? Mimi baba wako?*' meaning 'Why do you ask me for cigarettes? Am I your father?' He was so irritated that he stopped his intended search and went back upstairs while we resumed our work as futilely as before. We peeled paint and rust off one bar but made no impression on it.

The following day was the same, save for an hour's delay when one of the guards was brought downstairs as a punishment. Luckily he wasn't locked up in the cells but sat on the bottom steps smoking cigarettes.

After three days of cautious, strength-sapping and nerve-racking labour, one of the two bars began to bend, but only very slightly. Futhermore, the bar returned to its original position as soon as the pressure on it was eased. Then the diagonal base broke off, but fortunately nobody heard the noise. This made it easy for us to push the stand itself through the gap and get better leverage. Although this wasn't much progress we were pleased

61

and hopeful. It was enough to encourage us and bring smiles to most of our faces.

Shortly afterwards, disaster struck. The projector stand broke. Our hopes and smiles vanished, we cursed the day we were born. God had definitely forsaken us. But why? Ugandans are very religious. Twenty-two martyrs had been made saints only a few years previously. Then why did He punish us so much? We all agreed that definitely God was punishing *us* and not Amin's thugs. Was there any reason, then, why we should continue praying to Him? After some soul-searching we agreed to continue praying to Him because we were unsure exactly what He was planning for us. The stand, which had been our sole hope, was irretrievably broken. What was left? We were so bitterly disappointed that we were ready to give up. We remembered the bricklayers who'd never returned and wished fervently they'd reappear, but they never did come back. Nobody could eat that day, but some time in the night, after some reconsideration and reassessment, we sat together again and prayed. I led the prayers for God's guidance and prayed He would give us the strength and stamina and steadfastness to persevere.

The next few days were miserable. There was more killing and several of us were taken away for torturing to sign written statements implicating ourselves in treason cases. Life was becoming increasingly impossible. We thought of friends we'd been together with in the cell who were now needlessly dead. We recalled the late Galabuzi Mukasa, who had managed to smuggle in his automatic watch, the one we were using to tell the time. His tweed jacket was another constant reminder of his gentleness. Whenever Kasujja took the bandages off his wound he remembered the late Mutabazi who had taken out the stitches. Each one of us went over his last will and testament aloud, all of us worried at leaving our families without financial support.

'But I'm sure none of you feels as much sorrow as I do,' Kasujja said.

'Now Kasujja,' Nambale reprimanded, fuming, 'I've always said you're stupid but you've never accepted it. What is it this time?'

'Yes,' Kasujja replied confidently, 'I know exactly what I mean. Everyone here has parents or a wife and children to miss but I have no child and the child I'm likely to have is still unborn. Can you imagine leaving a pregnant girlfriend behind?'

Nobody laughed; we were too tense for humour. At last we agreed to continue with our night-watches while at the same time seeking a solution to our problem. Meanwhile, Mutumba counselled us to be extra-careful in whatever we did. Since the last public execution there seemed to be a tightening of security. There were many more soldiers on night duty and more regular rounds of the building.

Discipline improved. For example, the ordinary State Research employees no longer came downstairs to gloat, threaten or shoot at us as if we were a sideshow at a circus. Previously there had been some girls who came downstairs and Ssekalo had started an aquaintance with one of them. We asked him to establish more contact with her so that in time he could request her to smuggle us a hacksaw. The girls came down before dawn, around 5.30 a.m. During the next few days Ssekalo made a point of standing by the gate from 4 a.m. to 7 a.m. waiting for her. She came only once, and then her behaviour was so repulsive that Ssekalo made no real approach. We never saw her again.

Major Kimumwe had been quite wealthy and at the time of his arrest he'd been found to have about Shs 100,000 (approximately £1,000) in his car. He suggested that if we could find someone to contact his wife in their Kampala shop, she would send us a hacksaw. We could propose giving a total reward of Shs 1,000,000 (about £10,000). Whoever accepted our offer would take a note to Mrs Kimumwe, who would provide him with a hacksaw together with half the reward. The other half would be collected from her on the evidence of a signed note from the major acknowledging receipt of the saw.

Without Ssekalo's 'girlfriend' or the bricklayers there was only Lieutenant Sande Diobe, who had smuggled notes to my wife, but things had gone sour in our relationship. At that time I was better off avoiding him. When Sande had taken my notes, he had started behaving 'big', wanting to have authority over my car.

My wife was advised to avoid him as most Ugandan soldiers were notoriously unscrupulous. Once a soldier knew you had a car, house, furniture or even money his next move was to get rid of you and appropriate whatever of yours he wanted. Consequently it was imperative my wife and friends avoid Diobe before he took it into his head to ask for ransom money.

Sande, being a talkative bully, got drunk in the officers' mess and mentioned how he'd taken my note to someone in Amber House. This angered his bosses, and the following morning about 9 a.m. I was called out for interrogation about allegedly smuggled documents. I knew exactly what the authorities were after, but initially denied any knowlege of them. I was further tortured for my denial. I was asked whether I knew anybody in the State Research Bureau. I replied I knew Peter and Sande because we'd attended a meeting together in Lome, West Africa. They concentrated on Sande until I admitted I had sent a message to my minister asking for another clearance to leave the country as I'd been told my clearance wasn't acceptable. I sincerely saw nothing wrong with Sande taking the message. I innocently confirmed it to avoid more torture, but it was hell for Sande as that afternoon at 2.15 he was brought downstairs by the Entebbe boys together with the Nakasero Prison Adjutant who was tall and black. He, unlike his colleagues, looked humble and questioned me politely. From his reactions he appeared to see nothing wrong in what Sande had done. They left, but when I saw Sande the following day, he was in a raging temper ready to shoot me. Major Kimumwe's timely advice saved me. Sande blamed me for having reported him to his superiors. I tried to explain what had happened to me, but he shouted me down. Major Kimumwe beckoned me into a corner and suggested I avoid him and ignore his rantings. From that time on we were all wary of him and it was inadvisable to utilize him for our purpose. Our range of choices was shrinking rapidly.

It seemed that our hopes for escaping were diminishing by the hour. We made a pact that everyone should deny any knowledge about how the hole had been made. We vowed to swear we had found it there. Let everyone be tortured to death rather than admit having made it, since all indications pointed to our dying in the cell no matter what. We still continued with our prayers at least three times daily, and it was by God's grace that someone turned up at our gate and called out, 'Is there anyone here called Nambale?'

We kept quiet at first as we well knew such calls often meant death for whoever was called. The gentleman again called out for Nambale, and we studied him carefully. He was short and wore a white shirt and long khaki trousers. He certainly didn't resemble an ordinary Ugandan soldier.

Finally Nambale identified himself and they had a friendly talk. This was a relative of Nambale's who worked in the State Research Bureau. He'd been asked by Nambale's parents to trace the place where Nambale's body had been thrown, as they'd heard he'd been killed. The two became friends and Nambale gave him a letter to take back to his parents as proof he was still alive. The next day the relative came back with a long letter from Nambale's father together with more news from his wife. The friendship grew even stronger, which was good for our plan, and the man seemed eminently trustworthy. We asked Nambale to ask him, in a round-about way, whether he would be willing to bring us something. Nambale's relative said he would do anything to save us, short of endangering his own life. We waited excitedly for him to return as he'd promised, so that Nambale could discuss our plan with him after re-establishing that he wasn't spying on us, but he never came back.*

We asked each other what was wrong with our plan, was it that God didn't want us to escape or that Satan, for the first time, had overpowered Him? My friends abandoned all hope. It appeared that I was left to execute the plan, although I'd been brought into it reluctantly. I persisted with the idea, rolling it over and over in my mind without finding a solution. Everyone

---

* The eventual reappearance of Nambale's relative relieved us of some concern because we thought he might have reported us to his bosses. He told us he'd had to go home where he'd been delayed.

braced himself for an honourable death by the firing squad, saying, 'It's better to die bravely than like a coward,' but I begged them not to give up completely because death is the last thing that happens in life and it should come only at the very end when all alternatives have been tried.

13

HOURS OF DESPAIR

'What other alternative is left, Mr Kato? We've tried everything and nothing worked. We have to await death,' Major Kimumwe said, reasonably enough, for of course I had no alternative plan.

Yet I wanted their moral support, I didn't want to admit defeat. I still believe that where there is a will there is a way. That was a saying which had been drilled into me by my English teacher, Mr Waigulo, in 1949 when I was a child in Primary Two. He crammed English poems, idioms and sayings into our heads, much to our distaste, and used force to be sure we learned them. So learn them we did, to satisfy him as well as to avoid beatings. I remembered this particular proverb because he'd made a song of it every time he entered the classroom: where there's a will there's a way. It was not until I was in Junior Secondary School in the 1950s that I really appreciated what it meant. Determination could save us, it could achieve the near-impossible. I walked aimlessly around the cell thinking about what we might do next, and nothing came to mind.

'Mr Kato is thinking hard, possibly he'll find an answer to our problems,' Major Kimumwe remarked.

'You never know. If he finds one we might give him the title of professor,' Okech suggested.

All this time Kasujja was busily looking for bits of metal in the rubbish. Asked what for, he answered, 'I'd like to make a saw so that we can cut that bar.'

'Kasujja,' Nambale asked, 'are you really normal?'

'Of course I'm normal. You wait and see,' Kasujja answered.

I pleaded with my friends not to discourage him. I sat with him to help him grind and fashion his saw. It took several hours to make and when we tried it all it could do was rid the bar of accumulated dust. Nambale hooted with laughter.

'I told you that you're a fool, Mr Russian Expert, but you never believe me. Why is that?'

After this failure it wasn't easy to make another proposal, particularly as our spirits had sunk to a new low. Nevertheless I plucked up the courage to say, 'I've thought of another project.' Nobody troubled to answer. 'Gentlemen, I've thought of another project,' I repeated. This time Major Kimumwe looked up at me and Kasujja laughed derisively. 'Gentlemen, I'm not ready to give up my life as yet. Please, if only for my sake, listen to me.'

'OK,' Major Kimumwe said. 'But make it workable.'

'I suggest that we dismantle that projector head, take out the motor and use it to cut the bar.'

Almost everybody laughed.

'Where will we get the electric cable?'

'It's there,' I told them, 'in that refuse. Almost fifteen metres of it.'

'How do you propose to do it?' Ssekalo asked.

'Well, if we put one end of the cable into a light socket and the other on the motor with its head held against the iron bar, the motor head will eat away the bar as it rotates,' I said.

'This plan sounds fair, but can it work?' Okech asked.

'This voltage is different from that of the projector,' Ssendawula pointed out. 'This is 240 volts, whereas that one is 110 volts.'

'That's right, but what effect would that have on the motor or the system as a whole?' I asked.

Ssendawula explained the sole effect would be to burn out the motor very quickly.

'But, then,' I argued, 'since we have two motors, when the first one burns out we can use the second one.'

After a long debate, they were convinced. 'OK, but first try it out here,' Major Kimumwe directed.

With everybody's approval, Ssendawula dismantled the projector head, extracted the motor and handed it to me. 'Here you are,' he said. 'I wish you the best of luck.'

'We all need it,' I answered. I took the motor and removed the light tube from the ceiling. Ssendawula held one end of the cable in the light socket while I held the other end in my right hand and the motor in my left. My friends watched me connect the cable to the motor. I hesitated then made the connection.

It was disastrous; the noise was like that in a saw mill, and in my consternation I dropped the motor and stared at Ssendawula who was already laughing at me. Everyone thought the racket had been heard beyond the prison confines, in which case we could expect to be shot any second. We knelt and prayed so that at least we would be shot while praying. When after a time nobody had come down, we realized we were safe. Understandably we abandoned that plan because if the noise made by the motor alone was loud then when the motor head was put against the iron bar it was sure to double or triple. My friends were kind enough to respect my attempt, their remarks weren't too derogatory and Okech even encouraged me to think of another solution.

14

THE SECOND PROJECTOR, OUR SAVIOUR

The killing in the execution room on the ground floor still went on. It was galling to have to wait helplessly for our own deaths. I asked my friends to bear with me again. This time they were reluctant but eventually agreed.

I suggested that, as a last resort, we dismantle the second projector and try out the second stand, 'this time very cautiously'. Ssendawula was the leader of the opposition because, he said, we knew in advance it would break. After lengthy persuasion they agreed and we started our exercise all over again.

We went through the same routine of stripping the stand and inserting its base first. We pushed it for a full day without making any progress, except that the diagonal base broke off, enabling us to insert the column between the bars. This was taxing and tedious, but I managed to persuade my friends to continue each time they were about to give up. The lack of noticeable progress was demoralizing, but we persisted and also increased both our watchfulness and security because we knew one foolish mistake could cost us our lives.

We needed good cover but there had to be variations to make things appear normal. One cover was a game of draughts with beer-bottle tops. We always left it arranged in such a way that whoever came to check on us would find the pieces laid out on the board as if the game had begun a while ago. When Amin's thugs came down they found us deeply absorbed in the game and had no way of detecting that this was an act; it had to seem real if we were to survive.

Another cover was to rush to our allocated sleeping places and pretend we were either fast asleep or drowsing. The cigarette diversion was probably the best of all. Although only a few of us smoked we all pretended to, so that when one of us was given a cigarette we all shared it in the presence of the guard who'd given it to us. In most instances he would be amused and even laugh. The trick continued with the aim of pestering whoever came our way for cigarettes.

We also drew up our escape route. None of us knew exactly how the back of the building looked but we could see fencing through the glass louvres of the ventilators. Major Kimumwe also had some idea of the surrounding area. At the front of the prison was the French Embassy, and the Presidential Lodge was near by up the hill. We found we had three alternative routes.

The first and shortest, and on the face of it the safest, was to turn right after coming out of the ventilator and wriggle through the drainage pipes, which passed in under the entrance to the prison, to the other side of the road. The fear of encountering poisonous snakes or a total blockage, however, made it altogether risky.

The second route was to crawl around to the back of the building, climb the first fence, then go right around the front into the French Embassy grounds and out. The risk here was that of being seen by the guards in the front because we would be passing directly before them and the area was well lit.

The third route was to climb the fences immediately across from the ventilators, cut through a neighbour's compound, then out. The risks were that we had to climb several fences which could have strong electric currents; that the sentries, not far away from this position, might hear us; and, lastly, the neighbour might be the owner of the dogs which we often heard barking.

All these considerations made the final selection of our escape route difficult. We settled on the last one because the entire route was in darkness. We agreed to help Kasujja climb the fences.

This was all we could plan until the day came when Okech was ordered to take out our toilet bins. These were emptied behind the building and provided him with first-hand information on our intended escape route.

'How does it look out there?' we chorused on his return.

'It's all right,' he told us. 'There's a seven-foot wall at the end of the building and a number of fences, but the best route would be right in the corner where the wall is not so high.'

'What about the fences?' I asked.

'I don't really know; they're the usual chain-link ones but I'm not sure if they're electrified.'

'Well, I'm afraid we'll have to sacrifice someone,' Kasujja said. 'Whoever first touches the fence will be electrocuted and at the same time the fuses will blow. This will be an ideal opportunity for the rest of us to get out.'

'Why do you say "we"?' Nambale asked. 'Don't you know you're at our mercy, in fact you're a plain bother until we're outside those fences.'

The way behind the ventilator looked fairly clear, but what about that unyielding iron bar? After a week the bars still resisted our efforts and we were worried. Time was the vital factor. Even I, the most optimistic in the group, secretly began to despair although I concealed it lest they all throw in the towel. I tried to 'transplant my heart into their chests' to raise their morale. Repeatedly I reminded them of my English teacher's saying: Where there's a will there's a way; and time after time I begged them to persevere just a bit more, another few minutes and then a few minutes again.

'If we could only get hold of the blade of a hacksaw from somewhere,' young Kasujja persisted monotonously. This irritated us because it showed how childish Kasujja was. The proposal had already been exhaustively examined and found wanting. Furthermore, tempers were now running high. Everybody except Kasujja was doing his level best but the iron bar showed no sign of bending. Kasujja had already disappointed us by leaving his sentry post at the gate because, he said, 'there's no point in fighting on when there's no hope of success'. Immediately he realized how much he'd offended us and amended his view by saying he had thought of some other friends within the State Research Bureau who, if offered the reward originally planned, might assist us. After some deliberation, however, we decided the idea was too risky because they were Amin's tribesmen.

Then we wondered if it might not be possible to dig the bars out of the wall, provided they'd not been inserted too far. Ssekalo tried digging them out using spoons, nails and anything else he could find. This led nowhere. The deepest we could probe was about two inches, and this had no effect. We continued pushing the stand, hour in, hour out, but half-heartedly. At this junction Kasujja insisted on making another hacksaw, and I encouraged him. Keeping busy was essential. Major Kimumwe also helped him, and between them they produced a primitive and wholly ineffective tool. It was no better than the first one.

15

A RAY OF HOPE

Disappointed again and in a low spirits we decided to break off earlier than usual. In the afternoon we resumed and had worked for some fifteen minutes when the unbelievable happened. When we pushed the right-hand bar it didn't return to its upright position. It had definitely bent. Everybody jumped for joy and the stand fell out. God had performed a miracle. He had shown His power. He was alive and He was the Almighty. The impossible had been rendered possible. Major Kimumwe, who was at the ventilator, shouted exuberantly. Kasujja, who had resumed his gate duties, hopped on his one leg pretending to be exercising so that those in Cell 1 were not alarmed.

The very bar which we had not expected to give was the one that had bent. We tried to pass our heads through the gap created but at first none of them would go through. Even so, we were convinced we were almost there. The other bar now also was bent slightly. We knelt and said short prayers of thanks to God for showing us His power. We prayed also for forgiveness for the adverse words we had said about Him. We pushed the first bar further and further until all our heads could go through. It was an amusing sight to watch each of us putting his head through; everybody wanted to be sure he wasn't left behind when the others walked to freedom.

Nambale was to go first, then Ssendawula, Mutumba, Ssekalo, Okech, Kasujja, Kimumwe and myself. Because of my age and status, plus the position I had now acquired, it was important I took the leading role where necessary. Everybody was elated because we knew we could leave that night. Although no food was brought to us that day, we remained in good spirits. At 1 a.m., when zero hour arrived, we woke up, opened the hole we'd closed, took off our handcuffs and were ready to go. It came as a blow when Ssekalo's shoulders failed to go through. The hole was not big enough. We had worked under our childhood assumption that where a head can pass, the rest of the body can follow, but this was not so. Was it more hard luck? Or was God trying to show His power? Ssekalo's shoulders were too big to go through. Nambale and Mutumba couldn't get through either.

We decided to widen the hole the following morning starting at the usual time. We belatedly realized that shoulders can go through a rectangular aperture but not a circular one.

16

THOSE STUBBORN BARS

Around 9 a.m. we resumed work with renewed excitement, only to find the bars, having cooled down, would no longer bend. We stubbornly continued with our work until Kasujja alerted us to a 'rat' coming downstairs.

As usual he hopped around like a chimpanzee trying the cigarette trick but when this failed he sat down pretending to be in agonizing pain from his wound instead. He took off the bandage to expose the wound and flexed his thigh muscles, causing the wound to open up and close. This ugly sight was unbearable to the sentry who was pretending to be checking on our security. Kasujja asked him for pain-killing medicine, which further annoyed the guard. 'Stop that!' he shouted. 'I'm not a doctor, but even if I were I wouldn't give a scum like you any medicine,' and he stamped off angrily.

We used to tease Kasujja saying that as he only had one leg, it would be impossible to take him with us as he'd delay us and we'd all be captured. Hearing this, he made prodigious efforts to show us how fit he was and how nimbly he could move in spite of his handicap. Then we teased him again, saying that as he had only one leg he would be easily picked out even from a distance. After excitedly jumping around the cell, he suddenly dropped to the floor and did a perfect imitation of a dog walking on all fours. Finally we told him he had no hope of climbing the wall and getting through the fences between us and freedom. He replied by crawling all over the floor and leaping high into the air on his one leg. Then he told us not to worry about him as, if he failed to negotiate the obstacles, he'd chance the drainage pipes which led outside the State Research Bureau compound to a certain street near the Fairway Hotel. 'When I get to that street,' he informed us with a meaningful wink, 'I'll know where to go.'

Kasujja was courageous and talented. Once, when we were busy at our work, we heard him casually point out to someone the presence of a rat. 'There is a rat, *Efendi*.' The warning was rather belated. Possibly Kasujja's attention had been diverted by something going on in the other cell, because Amin's brother-in-law had reached the bottom steps unnoticed. He was a Muganda and the brother of Sarah Amin, currently the most loved of all Amin's wives. Tall and fat, he'd been given the task, probably because of his relationship with Amin, of taking down statements as prisoners were tortured. He was handsome and appeared to have a reasonably good education. Like all Amin's people he was a 'grabber' because one day he openly boasted how he'd taken someone's Citroën car by sheer force.

'Where's the rat?' he asked.

'It ran behind the staircase,' Kasujja replied smoothly, distracting him for a few minutes to give us time to hide our tools and take our positions.

When Mutebi, as he was called, came to our gate, Kasujja's quick mind slipped competently into gear. '*Efendi*, there's a new fellow here who is completely innocent. Maybe you can assist him by taking him upstairs to your office,' he said, meaning the torture room.

'Where is he?' Mutebi asked, then surveyed me with a look that clearly doubted my innocence. 'What did you do? Are you also a guerrilla?'

'No,' I said and explained the reason I suspected I was there.

Mutebi turned to Kasujja and said, 'You said he was *completely* innocent which means you, at least, are guilty of what you're accused of.'

'No, *Efendi*,' Kasujja contradicted confidently. 'What I meant was that in the case of an elderly and respectable gentleman like him, it would be too much to suspect he'd try to leave the country without proper clearance.' The conversation was becoming dangerous. '*Efendi*,' he volunteered, 'take me, I promise I'll be co-operative this time.'

'Isn't that what you always say? In fact, if you guys wanted to save yourselves a lot of torture you should just admit at once what we want from you,' Mutebi said. 'Anyway,' he added, 'I'll have a look upstairs and check on his file. Maybe he'll be smarter than all of you.'

When Mutebi returned a little while later, he had changed his attitude towards me and even evaded Kasujja's questions, but finally he unwittingly gave us a hint what the allegations against me were when he said, 'As for him, just let him rest comfortably, he's special.' He then took a prisoner from the other cell to his office.

Work at the ventilator continued until the right-hand bar had bent a little more. We thought now we could all get through and again organized ourselves for the escape. We awoke at 1 a.m. as usual and removed our handcuffs. We lifted Ssekalo above our heads and he pushed his head through the hole but it was obvious that it would take time and manoeuvring to get his shoulders to follow. This meant that Kasujja and Okech, who were built more heavily, would not be able to get through. A quick decision was taken to abandon the escape until the hole was wide enough for the broadest chest.

We whispered to Ssekalo to push himself back inside but, having tasted the outside air of freedom, he fought on to get his hips through. 'Ssekalo, Ssekalo,' we entreated, 'please come back,' but Ssekalo was struggling to get out. 'Ssekalo, Ssekalo, please, please . . .' but he was determined to get out and, unlike Noah's dove, leave us all behind in the cell. We seized his legs and forcibly pulled him back.

'Why did you pull me back?' he demanded angrily. 'We could all have got through.'

'What about us, you selfish bugger?' Kasujja snapped.

'This is not the time for recriminations,' Okech reprimanded.

'Ssekalo, please tidy up outside where your hands have been

playing about.' We lifted Ssekalo again so that he could push out one hand to smooth any incriminating marks; happily the soil was dry and marks were not conspicuous.

We further tightened our security and also slightly modified our cigarette trick. Now whenever guards came to check on us, we sent two or three people to the gate to confuse them with gabble and obstruct their view into the cell.

The keys of our cell were kept by a corporal called Ongolo, a Lugbara. We nicknamed him *'Wewe'* because he began almost every sentence with this Swahili word meaning 'you'. We soon learned how to deal with him. His sergeant was hardly ever seen and all the soldiers were loath to come into our cell because we stank abominably. In addition to the odours from our toilet dustbin, our bodies and clothes smelled to high heaven as we were never permitted a shower or bath. This was actually a blessing in disguise as it gave us the golden opportunity to work on our escape plan for long periods without arousing the slightest suspicion.

We were now convinced it would be only a short while before we gained our freedom. As things continued to improve we felt an intense excitement mixed with fear. The nearer we came to success, the more obvious were the results of our activities. The bend in the bar was by now so pronounced that it could be seen by the naked eye from quite a distance. To camouflage it, we had to be sure a concealing shirt always hung on an adjacent nail, and that folded sisal sacks were up in the ventilators. Normally, it was the prisoners in Cell 1 who collected our toilet dustbin, but realizing the increasing risk in letting them do this, we handed them the dustbin at our gate to forestall entry into our cell.

17

COULD IT BE THE ENTEBBE RAID?

One morning around 10 a.m. we heard someone come downstairs with keys. It was Mutebi collecting us for a torture session. We were taken in pairs. The first two were Ssekalo and Kasujja, who returned with swollen eyes and cheeks and bruises all over their bodies.

I was taken up alone and Mutebi announced my arrival by wordlessly pushing me into the torture room. This was about fourteen feet square and poorly lit. Two soldiers faced each other and a third faced me, by the door. All held whips. Mutebi sat at a small table and started asking me questions.

'Where were you going?' he inquired.

This was a stupid question because everyone knew the answer and I was puzzled, wondering what was wanted of me. The truth was no good, it had landed me in hot water some time back. If I appeased them by saying 'I was going to Tanzania,' I would merely hasten my death. While I was still deciding what to say the two soldiers rushed at me, shouting insults and beating me until Captain Yoswa, as I later learned the third soldier was called, ordered them to stop. The interrogation continued fruitlessly.

I had never been told what I was accused of, but I always suspected it was concerned with the Israelis' Entebbe raid. Later I was able to confirm this suspicion. This was the only serious 'offence' I could think of.

At the time the Air France Airbus was hijacked to Entebbe Airport, I was the Assistant Director-General of Civil Aviation in charge of air traffic services in all three states of the East African Community — Kenya, Tanzania and Uganda. I was stationed at the directorate's headquarters in Nairobi and was directly involved in the hijacking, as all reports had come to me first. On receiving the first news of the hijacking, I had immediately alerted all air-traffic control stations in East Africa, so that when the aircraft turned up at Entebbe, the Entebbe air-traffic controllers were aware of the hijack although they did not know its route, destination or position. When the aircraft finally landed at Entebbe Airport, President Amin started negotiating with the hijackers. During the hijacking ordeal I alerted the Uganda Air Force authorities, through my officer-in-charge at Entebbe Airport, to 'a remote possibility of an attack in an attempt to rescue the hostages'. I also asked him to make them appreciate the deficiencies of civil radar.

'I have done so,' reported Mr Fabian Rweigembe, the officer-in-charge, Air Navigation Services, Entebbe Airport. 'I've even told them of the possibility of jamming our radar and of enemy aircraft flying very low along the lake.'

'Have you stressed the point that they should not rely on us for the security of the airport?'

'Oh, yes,' he corroborated. 'In fact the colonel in charge of the airport has said: "Don't worry, it's the Big Man himself at the steering wheel. The situation is under control." So, you can see for youself, I couldn't have done better.'

'That's fine,' I approved, 'but I'm still not convinced they've thoroughly understood you. Please ensure our Entebbe radar is manned continuously. By the way, how's the radar at Katabi?'

'Well, no one really knows,' he replied, 'but it's probably all right — except that with the casual approach of our "friends" I wouldn't be surprised if their radar controllers were found in Kitoro during their hours of watch.' Kitoro was their favourite

81

place of amusement. 'All man's greatest evils — beer and women — are available in plenty!'

'Anyway,' I instructed, 'please keep the radar manned and be prepared for any eventuality. And keep us informed.'

18

THE NIGHT HELL FELL ON TO ENTEBBE AIRPORT

The night of 3 July 1976 was the night hell fell out of the sky on to Entebbe Airport. At about midnight, the Israelis, after flying some 2,000 miles from Tel Aviv, attacked and killed Amin's soldiers guarding the hostages and snatched the hostages away (except for one old lady who was in Mulago Hospital). It came as no surprise to me. When Mr Szredski, the duty air-traffic controller in the East African Area Control Centre, Nairobi, rang me up to express concern about the unusual telephone responses he was getting from the Entebbe control tower, I asked, 'Have the hostages been freed?'

'I'm not sure,' he answered, 'but there's certainly something funny going on at Entebbe because even the controller seems to be working under duress.'

'What about traffic in the rest of the East African air-space? Is the traffic into and out of Nairobi Airport normal?' I asked.

'Yes,' he replied.

'Then try to establish the facts and ring me back.'

The next ring was about an hour later.

'There are some B707 aircraft coming into Nairobi Airport but they, too, look funny,' he told me. 'When asked about their unusually slow speed and low level, the pilot said they have some engine oil leaks. On the other hand, the radar controller thinks the aircraft may be flying in formation.'

'Have you established contact with Entebbe?' I asked.

'No, but I'm still trying.' He rang off again.

The next call was about 2 a.m. 'There's definitely fighting at Entebbe,' he said. 'According to the Nairobi Airport controller, several aircraft have landed and some people have been carried away on stretchers.'

'I think you're right,' I said. 'The hostages have definitely been freed. Nevertheless, please try to obtain more information and keep me advised.'

I then rang my boss, the Director-General of Civil Aviation, to brief him. By six o'clock, several world radio stations had already broadcast the news of how the hostages had been rescued, but regrettably most people in Uganda, including the Director-General of Civil Aviation, the late A. Kalanzi, were unaware of this. I am the one who rang him up. At about 11 a.m. he rang me back to report that controllers F. Rweigembe, Mr Mawanda, Mr Muhindo and a few others had been arrested and taken to unknown destinations. He was all too obviously panicking. He said he was going to Entebbe to check, but half an hour later he rang to advise me he had decided to cancel the trip to Entebbe and to go into hiding instead, 'This is terrible,' he said – and those were the last words I heard from him until he came out of hiding several months later.

At about 11 p.m. on 3 July, someone rang the Entebbe control tower to inquire whether President Amin had returned from Mauritius where he had gone to hand over the OAU chairmanship. Control-tower staff are very well trained. Their training teaches them diplomacy and how to deal with media inquiries. Mr Muhindo, the controller on duty, tactfully referred the caller to the State House for an answer.

About an hour later an aircraft was seen landing on Runway 17 at the northern end of the airport. By instinct the air-traffic-control assistant, Mr Rukera, switched off the runway lights because, as he said later, he thought, 'We have been invaded.' When the runway lights were again switched on, there were several aircraft heading for the old airport, taxiing along Runway 12 where immediate heavy shooting broke out, on the northern

84

side. Possibly this was to distract the attention of Amin's soldiers, because in no time the airport seemed to be on fire.

'Let's run away,' Mr Rukera urged Mr Muhindo, the controller, but as a well-trained and conscientious controller, Mr Muhindo refused, saying he couldn't leave the control desk unattended.

'But call the air force officer at the gate,' Muhindo said.

When the air force officer, a lieutenant, arrived in the tower, he looked more puzzled and scared than they. He immediately ran back downstairs and Mr Rukera followed him to save his life. They were confronted by Amin's soldiers manning the tanks which had been stationed there for the protection of the air-traffic-control complex.

'*Unakwenda wapi?*' they called. 'Where are you going?'

'We have been invaded . . . invaded . . . please run . . .' Mr Rukera replied, but the soldiers didn't understand him, no doubt because of the language problem.

With great presence of mind, he went through the fence and hid himself in the cassava plantation around the complex. He watched the raid from there, constantly fearing the invaders would blow up the control tower and kill him, too. He remained hidden until noon.

Sometimes it's dangerous to stick to one's professional ethics. Muhindo was killed by Amin's infuriated soldiers because he stuck to the air-traffic-control rule of not leaving one's control desk under any circumstances until handing it over to another competent controller. Muhindo remained in the control tower until the following morning when he was picked up at daybreak by Amin's soldiers and taken for torturing.

The soldiers at the air-traffic-control complex had remained there half-heartedly because they were uncertain whether invaders had attacked the airport or whether this was the expected coup. Whatever they might have concluded is now immaterial, but the fact remains that they made no move whatsoever to counteract what was taking place down below. The air-traffic-control complex is on a small hill overlooking the whole airport, so that they were in an excellent position to shoot at invading aircraft.

Air-traffic controller Muhindo was a remarkably handsome young man of twenty-five, about five foot six in height, slim and of a light complexion. He was a gentle, soft-spoken person and a very good approach controller who had worked at several air-traffic-control stations in East Africa. He was married with one child. Before he was transferred to Entebbe Airport he had worked at Mombasa in Kenya. He had objected to the transfer because of the killings in Uganda. After making several representations against the transfer he turned up one day in my office early in the morning accompanied by his Kenyan wife who was pressing earnestly for her husband's transfer to be cancelled so they could remain in Kenya.

'Please, Mr Kato,' Muhindo begged, 'don't send me to Uganda because I'll surely be killed by those State Research Bureau fellows.'

In reply to my questions, he explained his fears, which were of a general nature. He had no specific reason to expect Amin's men to pick on him. I also explained my position. At this time the East African Community was badly shaken. Kenyan politicians were bawling at all Ugandans and Tanzanians to 'go home'. The East African Directorate of Civil Aviation, like most of the East African Community departments, had a number of Ugandans in the top positions. For example, the Director-General of Civil Aviation, Mr Z.M. Baliddawa, was a Ugandan. Out of the five divisions, three were headed by Ugandans.

Looking at the air-traffic controller's cadre, a high percentage were Ugandans, yet there were only two manned aerodromes in Uganda compared to about twenty in Tanzania and seven in Kenya. The politicians were deliberately being fed incorrect information by civil servants, particularly in Kenya where it was assumed that, if the community broke up, the Kenyans would divide all of the East African Community 'cake' among themselves as they claimed Ugandans and Tanzanians were unwanted parasites. According to them, Kenya paid to support the community while the remaining two partners shared the benefits.

The Kenyans in our directorate expected to replace the much-resented Ugandan personnel. The move to post East African

Community employees back to their respective states had been agreed upon in the East African Legislative Assembly. We were merely implementing the decision. We were being pushed, too. Therefore it was exceptionally difficult for me to post a non-Ugandan to Entebbe Airport. Although I fully appreciated Muhindo's fears, which I shared as a fellow Ugandan, I was in a fix. Services had to be provided. Ugandans did not want to return to their country. Non-Ugandans, in addition to having political backing *not* to be posted to Uganda, would see themselves as being sacrificed in place of Ugandans. As an administrator I had to take a decision.

'I'm truly sorry, Mr and Mrs Muhindo, because, although I understand your position, I'm afraid you have to go to Entebbe,' I summed up.

Mr Muhindo burst into tears and Mrs Muhindo reviled me. Then Mr Muhindo walked out of my office saying, 'OK, Mr Kato, let me go and die.' His wife slammed the door as they left.

The Israelis carried out their plan faultlessly with air cover and enough soldiers on the ground. The searchlight at the control-tower complex was also switched on, but we weren't sure who was responsible – very likely the Israelis. Amin's soldiers detailed to guard the air-traffic-control complex turned tail and ran, leaving their tanks.

When Amin's soldiers came to the control tower at about 7 a.m. on 4 July 1976, after the raid, they were in an ugly mood. They beat up whomever they found downstairs. They were thirsting for the blood of the air-traffic controllers who, according to them, had failed to keep the Israelis out of Ugandan airspace. Among those so senselessly beaten and left for dead was an office messenger. Mr Muhindo, still in the control tower, was waiting for his relief. They beat him up and took him along to look for more controllers. They went to Mr Fabian Rweigembe's house because he was the officer-in-charge, beat him up, put him in the boot of the car and drove off. The soldiers were on a maddened rampage looking for all air-traffic controllers.

At about 8 a.m. word went round that State Research officers were searching for all employees of the Directorate of Civil

Aviation. Several took to their heels while others found nearby hiding places.

Mr Rweigembe was as innocent as a newborn baby. He had warned them of a possible attack, he had told me only the day before he'd been to see Lieutenant-Colonel Orombi who was in charge of airport operations. Because our radar was not operating properly, he wanted the air force authorities to understand it could not be relied on at all and had made this amply clear. Lieutenant-Colonel Orombi had told him not to worry because everything was under control.

Born in Kigezi, western Uganda, Mr Rweigembe was a man of thirty-four, of medium size and weight, inclined to be hot-tempered but an outstanding administrator although some of his subordinates disliked him for his strictness. He insisted things be done to perfection. He had married only three months earlier and the films of his wedding were still in Nairobi where they'd been sent for developing and printing. It was I who had to collect them and send them to his widow.

Some officers hid in their ceilings, including Mr Mawanda who was picked up by Amin's soldiers around nine that morning. His wife Norah pretended to be sick but looking after her children. A house search was made and Mr Mawanda was found. He was shoved into the car boot and taken to an unknown destination. He was Number Two to Mr Rweigembe and a radar controller. A good person, he never picked quarrels, was quiet and had worked efficiently at all international airports in Kenya, Tanzania and Uganda. He was a great asset to the Air Traffic Services Division. He, too, was murdered.

Oluge-Awany didn't escape Amin's wrath, either. He'd come off duty a few days earlier and the news of the Entebbe raid found him relaxing with his family in a Kampala tourist hotel. Amin's thugs took him from his hotel room to an unknown destination. G. Baling Oluge-Awany was born on 6 February 1952 in the small village of Aluda in Olili sub-county, East Lango in northern Uganda. Coming from Lango, Obote's tribe, made him an obvious target for the Amin faction. Tall and black, he worked in the Directorate of Civil Aviation as a communications officer. His body was found in the Katonga River under the bridge along the Kampala–Masaka road. He left a wife and three children.

A number of people were picked up and killed while others simply disappeared. Some went into hiding and emerged later but Rweigembe, Mawanda and Muhindo were never found alive. It is probable they were taken for torture to the Entebbe State House where nails were hammered into their heads and their chests were pumped full of bullets. After several weeks of searching, their bodies were found in the Namanve Forest, only a few miles from Kampala along the Kampala–Jinja road. All their skulls had nails in them.

As already stated, it was highly dangerous to be found at any dumping place for dead bodies. Muhindo's body was buried by his colleagues in a shallow grave hurriedly dug in the forest because there was no possibility of safely transporting his body to his home. The bodies of Rweigembe and Mawanda were transported secretly to Kabale in Kigezi and to Kyaggwe in Buganda. Rweigembe had taken out a life-insurance policy, but because his body was buried without a death certificate and there was no police report, the insurance company was reluctant to pay the widow. Although it was risky, I went to Nairobi to make a declaration certifying his death as I felt a moral obligation to do this: Rweigembe was not only my officer but also a friend of fifteen years' standing.

While I was being tortured, this intervention came back to my mind as another possible reason for my arrest. Returned to our cells, we related our torture experiences. Major Kimumwe was almost strangled while Kasujja was burned on his back with match flames.

'But Mr Kato, you may be the luckiest of us all because the Israelis might feel obliged to help you when we reach Nairobi,' Kasujja pointed out.

'It's a bit too early to think about that now,' Major Kimumwe remarked.

Kasujja maintained that since I was tortured because of the Israelis, I might receive help from them. I was doubtful and explained how I'd been chased out of Kenya as a result of the Entebbe raid. From the information I had received in my capacity as head of air-traffic services I had been able to see nothing that could be remotely classified as Kenyan secrets, but the following day I was summoned to the Acting Director-General's office to give details of what had been logged in the Area Control Centre's log-book. My superior rang someone in the Kenyan government and spoke to him about the incident. From their conversation, which was in Kikuyu, I gathered that the Kenya government was concerned that a Ugandan knew the details. A week later I was told to 'stop coming to the office or anywhere near the building until further notice'. This was followed by a Kenyan government directive to all Ugandans to cease work in Kenya. Subsequently this was revised to affect only East African Community employees. All Ugandans, myself included, were sent on compulsory leave which, for most, lasted until the community was dissolved a year later. I was lucky in being posted to Uganda as Director of Civil Aviation. As my office worries and harassments were unknown to my family, they were anxious that I look for another job in Kenya rather than return to Uganda.

I considered Kasujja's idea more seriously. I had been harassed in Kenya to the point of being chased out of the country because the Kenyan government thought I might have passed on information to the Ugandan government. On the other hand, the Ugandan government was torturing me for not having alerted them to the Israeli raid. Kenya treated me as a spy, something totally outside my moral and psychological capacities. I'd lived in Kenya for fifteen years and suddenly I was treated as a spy. To the Ugandans I was a traitor. A traitor is the opposite of a spy. Certainly one of the two was wrong! In actual fact, both were wrong. I discovered much later from the guards that my arrest was the result of wild and malicious allegations made by irresponsible elements in my department.

Possibly Kasujja was right – the Israelis might be sympathetic to someone tortured for their sake. I wished I had acted one way or the other, spy or traitor, so that what I was now undergoing would be a fair punishment. God had started making miracles as He used to in the old days; perhaps He would influence His 'children' to remember me.

19

THE HOLE IS NOT BIG ENOUGH FOR ALL OF US

At last the bar of the ventilator bent further and we were sure we could all now get through. We rehearsed as before. At the appointed hour, we started the escape. This time we started with Okech, pushing his head out first, but his shoulders became wedged, and he couldn't get through although we pushed to the point of nearly breaking his collar-bone. He began breathing and groaning so deeply we feared he would be heard. So we pulled him back down.

The sentries must have suspected what was going on downstairs for one of them came tiptoeing to check on us. Kasujja was on guard at the gate and as soon as he saw the sentry's feet on the steps he signalled us to stop and lie down while he pretended to be using the toilet dustbin.

This sentry was a particularly dangerous fellow, short and obnoxious. I remembered him as one of those who had arrested me nine months before and had taken me to Makindye Military Barracks. On my discharge from there he had pretended to assist me in starting my Fiat car whose battery had run down. Although now fat, he had been slim at the time. After his pretence failed, he had attempted to take the car by force but fortunately the car was always difficult to drive after any period of standing still and after running for a kilometre it had stopped dead and he had been unable to start it again, so he had abandoned it. When I was first brought to Nakasero, I spotted him but ignored him. This was the fellow who now came down, checked on us, went halfway back up and sat on the stairs, listening to us.

We had by now identified good and bad shifts of our guards. Those who were 'good' went to sleep at 9 p.m. never troubling to look downstairs as long as the outside watch maintained its patrol. Our tiptoe guard belonged to one of the 'bad' shifts, silently coming down to check on us in the middle of the night. Perhaps this was how he'd earned his promotion to a full lieutenant. He had grown so enormous his waist seemed about to burst, his cheeks were puffed out and oversize, making his head look deformed, and his belly was like a pregnant woman's at full term. In his cunning way he would bring us drinking water when we were supposed to be asleep at three in the morning.

One of the shifts was Kibirige's. Kibirige was a fat, short Muganda, dark-skinned and remarkably kind to all prisoners. On a number of occasions he pleaded with his fellow guards to stop flogging prisoners. I felt he was forced into his job for monetary considerations and not for property stealing like the rest of the young men. He was a mature man aged thirty-five; his sole drawback was that, probably because he wasn't of Amin's tribe, he was most concientious about his job. He never took chances and he, too, frequently came downstairs. The rest of the shifts were average. Going by tribes, the Itesots were the best as they were indifferent, showing neither kindness nor malice.

The sentry came downstairs again, looked around and went up. We promptly held a conference to decide our next step. The thin ones insisted we attempt again and, if necessary, leave behind whoever failed to go through. Our unity was threatened. We now had three groups, the slight ones who felt imposed upon in having to wait, the heavies who insisted on sticking to our original decision and the medium, to which I belonged. We wanted to be fair to everyone. After a long debate, it was agreed (by majority vote) that we postpone our plan again until all were able to go through.

After more feverish work, the bar bent yet a little further and we thought that seven of us could make it; but a solution had to be found for dealing with the eighth. Either we escape leaving Okech behind against his will and so risk being shot while climbing the fence, or die like sacrificial lambs because of Okech's large size. Whispers from the slight group became more frequent and louder. We used a piece of string to measure the size of the hole against our shoulders. We also simulated our escape by leaving a gap between two old boxes on the floor. One of us sat on each box to keep it steady while the rest of the group wriggled through. We all went through except Okech. Sergeant-Major Okech's head could go through but not his body.

We continued to work frantically to increase the gap, but still the bars wouldn't give sufficiently. However, we were now confident the end of our ordeal was just around the corner. We calculated that soon there would be a presidential demand for some sort of confession. We decided that if the demand came before our escape we would write down what was wanted of us in order to avoid further unnecessary torture and so gain a few more days to work on the bars. Being stubborn or heroic would mean more torture and increased physical incapacity. The idea was unanimously agreed to, probably because the 'slight' group saw it as a means to an early escape.

I'm not unduly superstitious, but sometimes when events happen exactly as they are casually predicted without any reasonable pattern, trend or relationship, I admit to being puzzled. Maybe that's what's meant by 'prophecy'. According to my culture, it's bad to make statements implying negative omens, such as telling a pregnant woman she will give birth to an abnormal child. If, by bad luck, anything happened to her or the child during delivery or immediately afterwards lending credence to the statement, you would be outcast. It would be the general belief that you had contributed directly or indirectly to the misfortune, probably by witchcraft. In Buganda it is prudent not to make 'bad omen' statements, otherwise you could be branded a witch or a wizard.

It is my belief that the mere pronouncing of 'bad omens' does not necessarily invite or predict them. However, just after we discussed the matter, Kasujja, Ssekalo, Kimumwe and Mutumba were summoned by Major Faruk Minawa, the State Research Bureau's operations officer.

20

THOSE DEBILITATING TORTURE SESSIONS

Major Faruk Minawa claimed to be Ugandan, but was a Nubian from the Sudan who had settled in Bombo about thirty kilometres from Kampala. Broad and well-built, aged thirty-five and nearly six feet tall, his education had reached secondary-school level. Although Lieutenant-Colonel Itabuka, a Musoga, was the official head of the bureau, Faruk Minawa was the executive power and worked hand-in-glove with Amin on all its activities. It was quite usual for Amin to bypass senior officers and deal directly with his tribesmen however junior in grade they might be. Minawa was currently the number-one killer in Uganda. Black as charcoal and maintaining a frightening expression, his twitching eyes made his unappetizing face even more detestable. His protruding belly made him look nine months pregnant. His sadism was such that the only time he came anywhere near to laughter was when he watched a prisoner writhe and scream in dire agony. His function was to organize the beating and killing of important persons. He would watch, suggesting this or that method, and take a hand personally when his juniors showed signs of weariness or paused for a rest.

Fists, hippopotamus-hide whips, thick electric cables, torches in the eyes, metal canes, knives, hammers, fire between the toes, lighted cigarettes, broken soft-drink bottles for elbows and knees and sisal strangling ropes were all used in the torture procedures.

In spite of these no prisoner ever escaped the final gunshot or knife.

Once the prisoner whose turn to be tortured was before mine was ordered to stoop between two soldiers each holding a leather whip. As soon as his fingers touched his toes, the soldier behind him struck him and kicked him on the buttocks. The kick pushed him forwards towards the other soldier, whom he knocked over. This infuriated the soldier, who struck him heavily on the head. The two soldiers then continued methodically striking until they noticed their prisoner was unconscious. Minawa then ordered the soldiers to lift him by the feet so that the head dangled down.

'Now,' Minawa said, giggling, 'he'll be able to admit having planned to overthrow the government.'

During the few minutes this prisoner and I were together in the waiting room, we briefly told each other the story of our arrests. This prisoner was an old, respectable Muganda who had been a Member of Parliament. One day, after staying at a hotel in Kampala, he was tipped off about a plan to kidnap him. He took care to lock himself in his hotel room before dark, not opening his door to anyone and not answering the telephone to give the impression he was absent from the hotel every night. One night soldiers banged on his hotel door. From their talk he understood they had come to collect him but, as they heard no reply or any sound, they concluded he was still outside. They said they would wait until he turned up. He tore up his bedsheets, knotted them into a long rope, tied one end to the window sill and dropped the other outside. He climbed down from his room on the second floor, escaped to safety and went into hiding. But his hide-out was discovered. About 3.30 on a Saturday afternoon a taxi stopped at the gate of the house where he was hidden; four youngsters jumped out and swaggered into the house. They held him by the neck, beating and kicking him for sport before taking him to Makindye Military Police Headquarters where he was again beaten up; this time his right leg and arm were deliberately broken, simply because he had tried to resist the beating.

As he was an influential figure, pressure was put on the

military authorities to give him medical treatment. Meanwhile, everything movable in his house was taken by the so-called security officers who had arrested him. He was moved from Makindye to Mbuya barracks, then to Nakasero where we met. Although his broken limbs were still in plaster, they appeared to have mended. The accusation against him was that he had been working with anti-government elements. Faruk Minawa wanted him to sign a statement admitting this.

When he noticed the prisoner was unconscious, Minawa ordered him taken back to the cell and started on me. Mine was a random beating from Minawa himself. Realizing the amount of noise I was making, he asked whether the soldier had remembered to switch on the noise muffler, a diesel generator usually activated before torture began. This was surprising about Amin's thugs; one would not have expected them to feel self-conscious about their acts. Possibly they didn't want the French Embassy, next door, to hear corroboration of what the foreign press was reporting, which was distinctly adverse to the regime. Fortunately for me, the generator had not been switched on. Minawa lost interest in beating and ordered me returned to my cell.

Minawa was so powerful he could even order the torture of a soldier instead of a prisoner, if he suspected the soldier was trying to favour the prisoner under torture. Minawa had several wives and a number of children. One of his wives was the daughter of a prominent figure from western Uganda who had been a supporter of Obote and was a successful businessman. Despite this, Amin had offered him an important portfolio – although this did not make him immune from Amin's wrath as he was tortured and saw the inside of Amin's prisons on a number of occasions. This was yet another proof that Minawa knew no shame, because it would be normal for anyone to do everything possible to avoid the humiliation of one's father-in-law. He often brought his young children to the prison; we could hear them playing upstairs in the very area where people had been killed the night before.

Minawa's torturing followed a set pattern. He would order prisoners to be given a shower before interrogation. They were then brought into his office one by one, ordered to sit on the carpet and write out a statement to Minawa's liking, using pencil, pen, paper and a small table provided for the purpose. On several occasions the notorious Palestinian interrogator, nicknamed 'Faizal of the Nile', would be present. The torture either followed Minawa's lecture or preceded it. The degree of torture depended on a particular prisoner's willingness to admit to the stated crime.

21

WE CONFESS OUR GUILT

When my friends Kasujja, Ssekalo, Kimumwe and Mutumba were summoned to Minawa's office they went through the same routine. Faizal of the Nile was there and Minawa gave them his usual lecture, although this time it was longer than usual. He detailed what he wanted each to write. To his surprise, the prisoners wrote almost exactly as indicated. (This was, of course, because of our earlier agreement.) They even elaborated a little to make Minawa happier. After listening to their individual statements, he ordered them to sign them, then laughed and said, 'Very goo-ood!' He was definitely delighted with his achievement. 'If you'd been as co-operative before, you wouldn't have been tortured, but now look at all those scars on your bodies. You wouldn't have had them. I will make arrangements for you to see the president, who will pardon you. He'll pardon you for having been so willing to speak the truth freely.'

He called out for Corporal Ongolo and instructed him that, from then on, all our food was to be brought from the Standard Hotel and that we were to be given both breakfast and afternoon tea from the same source, which also supplied the State Research officers.

Everybody was excited but for opposite reasons. Minawa and his fellow thugs were excited because of their success. All troubles were over, admissions had finally been made and Amin would have another opportunity to prove to the world's foreign press that those killed by his regime were self-confessed traitors. This would earn promotions for Faruk Minawa and his colleagues and the prisoners would be disposed of by the next firing squad. Minawa sat smiling and mumbling to himself as if in a glorious dream. Aloud he said, 'Now all these months' work is over, the battle is won and you're my friends. Nobody will beat you again. If you have any complaints, make them straight to me and I'll make sure they're sorted out.'

The prisoners, on the other hand, were excited because Minawa's satisfaction heralded their clear escape. They knew that the guards would now be relaxed, to our obvious advantage. Watching Minawa's acts of indulgence, which were most unusual, the prisoners became even more intoxicated with the hope of imminent freedom. With the knowledge of our ventilator always in our minds, whatever horror the immediate present brought seemed immaterial. Everyone was even prepared to stand up and shake hands with Minawa to bid him farewell.

Everybody misses opportunities at some time or other, of course. Sometimes they pass without much regret, but Kasujja could not allow such a golden moment to slip by without saying something. He hopped up to Faruk Minawa. *'Efendi,'* he said, 'we are also very pleased with your offer and are willing to co-operate even further. Personally, I can add to what I told the president on the day of my arrest. However, I have a small request. Could we have some cigarettes, because whenever we ask for any the soldiers want to beat us.' Minawa promptly granted the request, passed out cigarettes and promised to make arrangements for us to see the president as soon as possible.

While we rejoiced at having scored so highly with our performance, we were all aware that the signed statements incriminated us to such an extent that no forgiveness was in any way feasible. As zero hour approached, we became increasingly concerned about the unknown area behind the State Research Bureau building which we would be traversing once out of the ventilator. If the fences were electrified, one or two of us would have to be sacrificed to enable the rest to escape when the fuses blew and broke the circuit. We couldn't expect a danger-free route.

101

From Major Faruk Minawa's windows my friends had had a good view of part of the grounds behind the building. Another opportunity for reconnaissance had come when we were all called out to push a stalled trailer. The trailer, belonging to a Somali trader, failed to start because the battery had run low. It was confiscated and allocated to one of Amin's thugs. While outside, we covertly studied the crucial corner. Annoyingly enough, and as if they had an inkling of our intentions, the guards sent one of their number to sit by the corner facing us as we pushed with maximum slowness at the vehicle and memorized every detail we could. When we had finished pushing, Ssekalo idly picked up a three-foot-long iron bar which he was determined to take with him into the cell and so solve Okech's problem. It took considerable persuasion to make him relinquish the idea.

We now believed that after all the setbacks we were as ready for our escape as we could ever be. We could accurately determine where most sentries would be at any given time. It was a matter of choosing the best way. Our initial choice had been Thursday, 15 September, which was the Moslem feast of Idd-ul-Fitr, the conclusion of Ramadan, the month of fasting. This would have been an ideal time, for the guards would be drunk and security inside and outside greatly relaxed. It would have been comparatively easy to mix with the celebrating crowds. But on that day the ventilator still resisted our efforts.

Now we learned Amin had ordered a twenty-four-hour stand-by at Nakasero of the two mechanized brigades of Malire and Marines. To us, the stand-by signified a late retirement by the night guards and additional rounds of the building. The general indication was that a coup to overthrow Amin's government was again in the offing, hence the sudden precautions. Another reason was that Amin feared some violent reaction to the many executions of innocent citizens after the Archbishop Luwum murder. For whatever reason, the move was not in our favour but we had passed the point of no return in our plans.

To give veracity to their signed statements the Kimumwe group had, in addition to telling deliberate lies, given general reasons for public discontent with Amin's regime: the continued

102

killings of innocent Ugandans by military personnel and the consequent brain-drain of professional men to other countries; the promotion of people in all sectors of society on a tribal basis irrespective of their education, experience and capabilities, which led to the dominance of the Kakwa and Lugbara tribes at the expense of efficiency; the lack of educated officers and administrators in the armed forces; the acute shortage of salt, sugar, soap, cooking oil and several other essentials except in the Kakwa, Lugbara and Nubian areas and the consequent black market and price inflation for these goods and the resultant worthlessness of Uganda's currency and the collapse of law and order and its replacement by military whim.

22

AT AMIN'S CAPE TOWN VILLA

Although Minawa had simulated satisfaction with the statements, some of them nettled him and, as expected, didn't please the president. The result was an order for four prisoners – Kimumwe, Ssekalo, Mutumba and Kasujja – to report to Amin immediately. At about 2.30 p.m. on 20 September, Amin's personal bodyguards came to collect them.

We were working on the ventilator as usual when Kasujja called out '*Mmese*' and hopped energetically about the gate while we, as always, took up our predetermined positions. We heard several steps descend the stairs in a great hurry, which didn't give us time to close the gap, but we managed to pull out the projector stand and hide it in the left-hand corner nearest the gate.

Kasujja launched into his invariable request. '*Efendi, tunataka sigara!*' meaning 'My lord, we would like some cigarettes!'

The soldiers were displeased and ignored Kasujja's request, and his quick wits alerted him to something unusual in the soldiers' manner, so he refrained from insisting. The soldiers had brought new clothes. They opened our gate, calling out for the four prisoners wanted by the president. Each was given a new shirt and a new pair of long trousers. After dressing they were rushed upstairs, bustled into waiting cars and taken to Amin.

We were initially thoroughly scared, thinking the soldiers would come into the cell and see our precious ventilator, but when they selected the four prisoners we were relieved – until we started worrying about where our friends had been taken and for what purpose. The fact they'd been given new clothes ruled out execution. If additional statements were wanted they would have been sent to shower to cleanse themselves of the maladorous prison stink.

They subsequently told us how the four of them were ordered to squeeze themselves on to the back seat of an old Datsun 160J sports car. The officers got into two other cars and off went the convoy, Major Faruk Minawa with a female secretary leading the procession. The new clothes convinced the four they were to see Amin and then undoubtedly would be taken to their deaths in the Namanve Forest.

After passing through the city centre on to the Gaba road via Nsambya barracks, they were suddenly at Amin's Cape Town Villa. Faruk Minawa left his car and approached the prisoners smiling broadly. He announced he had fulfilled his promise to fix an appointment for them to see President Amin, who would set them free.

'If you remain as co-operative as you've been lately, and are lucky, the president will set you free,' he said, stressing 'lucky'. 'All you have to do is elaborate on your statements. Please don't deny anything you've already said. If you go against my advice, don't hold me responsible for what happens to you.' He laughed boisterously and moved nearer to the prisoners, who had been ordered out of the car and stood in pairs, handcuffed. He patted Kasujja on the back. 'Remember your promise?' he asked. 'Be sure you fulfil it.'

'Yes, sir,' Kasujja replied. 'But sir, I would like a stick to walk with.' Despite Kasujja's one leg, he was denied this and had to depend on his partner for support.

Faruk Minawa then joined a group of senior military officers a few yards away. This group included Colonel Juma Oris (a Kakwa and a Moslem), the Minister of Information and Broadcasting and also, since the execution of Lieutenant Colonel Erunayo Oryema, the Minister of Minerals, Lands and Surveys and additionally, since the departure of Wanume Kibedi and Princess

Elizabeth Bagaya, Minister for Foreign Affairs. Also present was Lieutenant Colonel Juma Ali 'Butabika' (a Kakwa and a Moslem), the commanding officer of the Malire Mechanized Regiment at Bombo. Short and small, he was very powerful. Butabika is the national mental hospital and Juma Ali was so nicknamed because he was crazy. He was the chairman of Amin's military tribunal, which rubber-stamped Amin's death sentences, and was also Major Kimumwe's former commanding officer. He looked as enraged as a wounded buffalo, obviously impatient to receive the prisoners at his tribunal. Despite his small stature, he was a bully and constantly challenged far more strongly-built men – until the day he challenged someone who lifted him by the ears and dropped him into a puddle. A third member of the group was Captain Ondoga, Chief of Protocol, another Kakwa and also a Moslem.

The officers appeared puzzled and uncertain what to do with the prisoners. An order was issued to conduct them around the peninsula to impress them. The whole place swarmed with sentries, patrol boats zoomed on the lake and soldiers in and out of uniform busily scanned both the air and land area. It looked as if an invasion was expected at any moment. Suddenly Amin came out, strode about pointing at a beautiful home across the lake and hurried back inside. It transpired that the house was so placed strategically that he considered it a danger to his security and ordered it to be 'acquired' by the State House.

The prisoners were obliged to assume an air of gratitude for the beautiful tour they'd been given. The soldiers guarding them repeatedly pointed out the luxurious charms of the place. Meanwhile the prisoners were mentally rehearsing their next performance, how best to behave before the president. Kasujja was stage-manager and it was agreed to put on a 'don't care' attitude (after all, the ventilator was ready and freedom was only hours away, provided Amin sent them back to their cell). Kasujja was cautioned not to overdo it, not to be too carelessly indifferent.

The long wait of two and a half hours passed unnoticed. Amin was occupied in haranguing groups of lawyers and church leaders. It was during these harangues that he cleverly organized the resignation of the Sheikh Mufti, Mr Matovu, from the leadership of the Moslem Council. Although the official reasons given were medical plus misappropriation of funds from Saudi Arabia for the new mosque in Kampala, the actual reason was to replace him (a Muganda) with a Kakwa.

Around 4.30 p.m. the prisoners were escorted by Mr Ondoga to see the president, walking very slowly because it had been previously arranged that Kasujja should grossly exaggerate the pain in his half leg to try to win admittedly unlikely sympathy from the president. Walking in pairs, led by Mr Ondoga and followed by armed soldiers, the prisoners entered a circular room, twelve feet in diameter, and faced President Amin seated at the northern end. The room was some ten feet high with a pillar in the centre. At the southern end were Amin's henchmen: Faruk Minawa, Ali Juma 'Butabika' and a woman from the government-owned newspaper, the *Voice of Uganda*. Mr Matovu (another Matovu), the Minister of Justice, sat by the door wearing a grey suit with a big tie and looking as if he had no part to play in the proceedings. Possibly this was because he felt out of place as his part of swearing in a judge from Pakistan had just been concluded. On the other hand, Amin's intention might have been to legalize what was about to take place. Matovu was a medium-built lawyer who had risen from the rank of Solicitor-General to that of Minister of Justice in one of Amin's frequent vertical shifts of top civil servants. He was unambitious and listened woodenly to Amin with folded hands. Fear of his boss was his consuming emotion; even the prisoners' entrance seemed to hold neither interest nor significance for him.

23

FACE TO FACE WITH THAT MONSTROUS GIANT . . .

Ondoga moved to one side and, at last, the prisoners came face to face with the huge 140-kilo bulk of this monstrous man they had wanted – and still desperately wanted – to kill. He shouted at the prisoners to move nearer to him and ordered the cameraman to take shots for the national television news programme that evening. He then turned to the prisoners and produced all the English he knew, mixing it up with Swahili and Luganda and changing his mood with every pause. He wanted to impress them with his fluency in English and in fact remarked he was using better English than even that spoken at Oxford or Buckingham Palace. He was acting with his whole body, banging the chair arms with his powerful fists (he was a former boxing champion) and stamping the ground like a female buffalo protecting her calf. At times he seemed to smile, but it was not a smile. Was it the bitterness of his mind forcing itself out of his face? At other times he expressed anger. This was complete anger. His whole body shook and he made as if to grasp the prisoners and either stamp on them or strangle them. He then stood up and made a move as if to shoot them there and then. Then he paused for several minutes as if meditating and took a few slow strides across the room.

During this tirade the prisoners were frightened and showed it. Even cheeky Kasujja jerked backward, tugging at Mutumba to whom he was handcuffed. The movement caused Amin to look at Kasujja and say, with tongue in cheek, 'You may go if you wish.' Then, addressing Ondoga, he added, 'Open up their handcuffs. *Nza ayagala kulaba omu omu,*' meaning he wanted to see each one standing by himself.

The ensuing pause helped reduce the prisoners' panic while they stood quietly listening to this consummate actor. Eventually the torrent of abuse lessened and Amin seemed to cool down a bit. He beckoned Major Kimumwe with his pistol. 'You are the one who organized and supervised the killing of all the Acholis and Langis around Kampala. Why did you do this? Tell me now. You wanted to finish off all the Acholis so that the world would think "Amin is a murderer".' Turning to the journalist he asked, 'Have you copied that? This fellow wanted to spoil my name but I don't fear anyone except God. I knew I would get hold of him soon.'

The journalist replied affirmatively but looked sideways at his colleague behind the camera as if to say that Kimumwe's death sentence was on the way as it was common knowledge that Amin always transferred his personal responsibility for the rampant executions of innocent people to others. From past experience, Major Kimumwe had little hope of remaining alive.

Turning back to Major Kimumwe, he blurted, 'I trusted you too much!' He paused dramatically. 'I thought you were capable of commanding a force.'

Of course this was true. Precisely because of Major Kimumwe's abilities he'd been named one of the key plotters. After realizing that his statement could be misinterpreted to mean the opposite of what he intended, Amin continued, 'But I do not mean a commander should kill me.' He switched to Swahili. 'Because of this trust I appointed you the adjutant of Malire Regiment after which I promoted you and appointed you second-in-command of the same regiment.' He looked around, asked to see Juma 'Butabika' (Kimumwe's former superior) and turned back to Kimumwe. 'You fool! Instead of commanding a force to capture Cape Town, you planned to kill me! I will give you something that your friends will never forget. I was going to promote you into Juma's position to become the commanding officer of Malire. With all these facilities to make yourself popular and *mafuta-mingi* [a tycoon], what made you mad?'

'But, Your Excellency, I did not . . .' Kimumwe attempted to reply, but Amin suddenly whirled to berate Mutumba.

'You remember when we went to check the Mutukula border together? You remember how we threatened Nyerere and his boys? You were one of my favourites. I like you because you're a revolutionary. You've been a very good pilot and also an excellent instructor. Why do you think I gave you those promotions? It's because I trusted you that I gave you those big and responsible positions like being the adjutant of the Gulu base and being second-in-command of one of the fighter squadrons. You're still young, and if you're released now I'm sure you can resume your flying career and do even better in the future than in the past. You remember when I came to Gulu? Your officers and men trusted you implicitly. What made you turn against me? What more did you want? Did you think those people you're working for would ever give you better things? You fool!

As he spoke he appeared to become distracted by Kasujja's jerks which were the result of standing too long unassisted on one foot. His attention now turned fully to him and he said angrily, 'You, cadet Majwala, calling himself Kasujja. I'm the one who saved your life. You remember my soldiers were about to shoot you dead when I intervened? Can you remember the promise you gave me?' Kasujja moved as if to reply and at the same time assume a more comfortable stance but Amin barked at him to stop fidgeting. 'You remember I promised you you'd be all right as long as you told me the whole plan and showed me where all those who have guns now are? I think your leg can be worked on to enable you to resume flying. I can order a new leg for you this minute and you'll receive it immediately. Don't you know that I'm very powerful? But what else did you want? I'm the one who sent you to Russia where you learned how to fly helicopters and I was planning to make you my pilot! Why did you turn against me?'

Kasujja asked for permission to sit down, then said, 'Your

Excellency, sir, I will keep the promise. I will try to give as many details as I can remember but I'm not sure whether the gunmen are still where I left them.'

This in no way impressed Amin who turned to Sergeant Major Ssekalo. 'You are one of those I personally recruited in the Obote regime together with . . .' he hesitated but before he could mention names, Ssekalo spoke.

'Together with that minister seated there, Colonel Juma Oris. Most of those I joined with are now ministers or high-ranking officers and colonels.'

This pertinent remark momentarily quietened Amin, then he laughed a little, probably because Ssekalo's bold counter-attack so fully supported the accusations of tribalism. Regrettably for Ssekalo, he didn't come from the 'right' corner of the country. Had he come from West Nile, like Amin and his henchmen, instead of Buganda, he would by now have been a major, at least.

24

. . . WE HAD PLOTTED TO KILL

Ssekalo's remark excited the volatile Kasujja who, with escape via the ventilator in mind, burst out: 'Your Excellency, sir, as I said, we had hatched up a v-e-r-y good plan which I intend to disclose to you with full details. We wanted to start with your vice-president and move on to other self-styled governors like Nasur. In fact, if it hadn't been for that sergeant who betrayed us, by now you would be dead!'

This deeply annoyed Amin who started fuming. He said he could not believe the man mentioned was a traitor, because to him the prisoners were obviously the traitors. The sergeant in question was a Sergeant Dick who was attached to the air force. 'Dick' was not his name at all but he'd been so nicknamed because he was fond of using the English phrase 'every Tom, Dick and Harry' for anyone he didn't know. He was half Muganda, half Munyarwanda, his mother having come from Rwanda. Dick was talkative, especially after a few litres of beer, the sort of fellow not to be trusted with money because of his greed for it. His ability to keep secrets was also doubtful as he was too anxious to please his superiors to win favours and promotions. Additionally, being a womanizer, he could easily trade a top secret for an attractive girl's capitulation. It is believed this officer let the cat out of the bag just before the bullets were to go through Amin's chest by the cemetery, a mile from Entebbe Airport. This is where Amin was to have been ambushed, but somehow he got to know about the plot and deviated from the arranged route.

Soldiers were sent to catch the 'traitors', but unfortunately for them the traitors' communications system worked so well that none of them, except of course Kasujja, was arrested. All others sped away. Sergeant Dick was praised, especially by the Entebbe base commander, for having saved the country from bloodshed. The commander, in his broken English (he was illiterate, having been an unschooled lorry driver), announced a promotion for Dick to the rank of lieutenant.

Amin didn't want to discuss Dick, and started attacking some of the men he knew had been involved in the plot but who managed to escape to Nairobi. He accused Major Anthony Bazalaki and Lieutenant Willy Kimumwe of having run away with his MiG 21 and a MiG 17 respectively. Major Bazalaki, a slender man of about thirty, was a Christian from central Busoga who had joined the army in 1968. Willy Kimumwe was Major Patrick Kimumwe's brother and, like Patrick, quiet and reserved. Aged about twenty-five, he had joined the air force about five years earlier. They were both excellent pilots, which is undoubtedly why they had been recruited into the plot. The confidence they inspired in their colleagues gave them a place among the inner circle of men who held crucial responsibilities for the coup. When they received a tip-off from their intelligence system that Amin had taken a different route, they realized at once he had been alerted and Anthony and Willy headed at speed for the Kenya border. Because they were still in uniform they were able to bluff soldiers manning the road blocks on the way. Amin's intelligence system was operating equally efficiently and their car registration number was sent to the border road blocks. They would have been arrested had they not decided to use their superior guns to shoot their way past the last road block before the Kenya border.

'I'll get those fellows, too, and when I get them I'll bring them here,' Amin concluded. Then he glared at the prisoners and shouted at them. 'You'll have to pay for all this! As of today I've signed an instrument by which I'm going to hand you over to Lieutenant Colonel Juma. He is going to be the chairman of the military tribunal you're soon going to face. And,' he added ominously, 'if you're found guilty you'll go before a firing squad and be killed by your own guns, those you imported from Tanzania to kill me and my ministers.'

Kasujja suddenly stood up on his one leg and said, 'But, sir, ours were not from Tanzania. We got ours from our fellow Kakwa soldiers and they're of Russian make. Your Excellency . . .'

'Stupid!' Amin interrupted. 'The guns we captured and displayed to the public were big and most of them came from China. This time we don't want to take chances. Last time we used small guns and some stubborn boys almost saved their own lives as a consequence. My soldiers had to use many more bullets to kill them. You'll be shot by bazookas so that I can see what your bodies look like in pieces. On the other hand, you can save your lives by pleading guilty and letting me know the names of your friends still at large. If you do this, I'll instruct Colonel Juma, whom you see sitting over there, to set you free.'

He then calculated a longish pause as a preacher does to assess how much of his lesson has been assimilated. The pause was intentionally long enough for them to come forward, precisely as new converts would to confess their sins.

'Have you refused to plead guilty?' asked Amin. 'I repeat, if you wish you may plead to me for clemency and probably I'll forgive you because I don't want to lose courageous soldiers like yourselves. You know very well I can make the whole world tremble. Can't you remember how I even made the Queen of England kneel before me in Arua? If I can do that then what can stop me from releasing you?'

Amin was not a fool as has sometimes been thought. He was very intelligent but, due to lack of any basic education, most of his methods were crude. Pomposity was one of his attributes and when he had an opportunity to steal the limelight on the world's stage he didn't pass it by. When he had the chance to get hold of Dennis Hills, an English university lecturer who had referred to him in his newly-published book as the 'pumpkin', he not only threatened to kill him but made every move to show he was determined to do so. Emissaries and radio messages were sent to him from all over the world, appealing to him to spare the Englishman's life. Because world powers engaged themselves in such appeals, this proved to him he was one of the most powerful people living. The Queen of England was, to his mind, no exception. Through the then prime minister, James Callaghan, General Blair was sent to Kampala to negotiate with Amin at the eleventh hour. General Blair was selected because, at one time before Uganda's independence, he was Amin's senior officer in the King's Rifles (5th KAR). The British hoped that, using tact, the general could renew his personal friendship with his former non-commissioned officer, now a self-promoted general. With that advantage he might be able to secure the release of his fellow Briton. Again as if to prove his power, Amin made certain the negotiations took place in a tiny grass hut in Arua town where, Amin later claimed, the general knelt to him before starting talks. His reference to the Queen kneeling before him related to this incident. The British tactic worked – Dennis Hill was set free – but Amin's objective had also been attained.

Amin, continuing his effort to wring admissions from the prisoners, now said, 'You are my friends and I want you to go back to your units to serve this country properly as you had been doing.'

He ordered them to be escorted outside but, as they were being led away, they saw Faruk and Colonel Juma whispering to Amin who then requested several of his officers to remain behind. Because of the bluff they'd been treated to before and during the 'act', the prisoners were worried that the officers were either pleading for their release or for another 'act' directly involving the officers, in other words, another bout of torture. Whatever the whispering might have been about, the prisoners never knew as Amin emerged and ordered their return to their cell. 'But take them around Kampala, let them see how the shops are full of essential goods. Take them up to the suburbs,' he directed, 'they'll see what stocks have come in during the last three months while they've been in prison. Don't forget the Nakasero market.'

25

THE KILLERS HE RELIED ON

They were rushed into the waiting car and driven off. It was 6 p.m. and most of the shops were closed. The whole town looked deserted and the Nakasero market was shut. After the market they stopped at Sergeant Major Simba's bar on Bokasa Street. Simba, a tall, black man, was a Kakwa and a Moslem and the chief executioner at Nakasero. It was his car that was being used for the prisoners' transport. The driver left the car, entered the bar and, after a while, was escorted back by Simba who staggered and spoke loudly in Kakwa. The driver got into the car, Simba slammed the door and the prisoners were driven back to the prison and their cell.

The chat between their driver and Simba had made the prisoners uneasy. It couldn't have been about the pending tribunal proceedings, as Simba was not concerned with those found guilty by the tribunals. His duty was to kill and dispose of anybody brought to Nakasero, whether guilty or not. Possibly the chat was to alert the chief executioner to report for duty that night to finish off some stubborn prisoners who had dishonoured the president by refusing to plead guilty. It was disconcerting and unnerving.

Amin's government was based on tribalism and where this was not operative (when only Kakwas or Nubians were concerned), 'merit' was applied. Merit at Nakasero meant ability to kill and Simba was the expert at quick killing by knife, ropes and gun. It was because of this expertise that he'd earned himself promotion to the rank of sergeant major. His real name was Odul and he was born at Luwero in Buganda. His friends called him 'Wodi' and his Christian name was Peter. Because he was tall and hard-working, his colleagues at the cotton ginnery where he had formerly been employed during the cotton season nicknamed him Petero Mulefu (meaning Peter the Tall One). When he left Luwero to come to Bombo, the seat of the Nubians in Uganda, he became interested in State Research activities. He saw illiterate young Nubians owning big American cars and having bags of money. Money was no problem to them. Girls flocked to them, chiefs, civil servants and even policemen were at their mercy. They could arrest and kill with impunity, and demand – and get – tens of thousands of shillings as ransom.

Petero Mulefu thought he'd be an ungrateful fool if he, too, didn't jump on the band-wagon. One of the conditions of belonging to the privileged group was that he completely forget his identity and become a Nubian. This was no problem – he happily changed his name to Mohamed bin Abdala, born at Bombo. He also chose an official nickname for disguising his true past, another understandably common practice in the State Research Bureau. He picked 'Simba', as a step to becoming more Catholic than the Pope, in this case killing more people than even the Nubians themselves. Simba is the Swahili word for 'lion'. The former Petero Mulefu wished to be as fearsome as a lion and to be referred to as the king of 'the boys'. From fieldwork, Simba was posted to the headquarters of the bureau at Nakasero, which signified less material benefit for him as there were so many big bosses at Nakasero and all of them had to have their share of the loot. The compensation was that there were more killings at headquarters than in the field, which gave him a splendid opportunity to prove his worth as Simba, king of the jungle. He took care that his work was recognized by the bosses, especially Faruk Minawa, and as a well-earned result he was promoted to the rank of sergeant major.

Kakwa Moslems and Nubians were highly superstitious. They feared the spirit-revenge of the innocent people they killed. As a

117

means of suppressing the spirits' anger it was common practice for the killer to eat raw parts of the body he had killed, so that many of the bodies found in Uganda under the Amin administration had liver, heart, eyes, ears, breasts and genitals missing. For Simba to prove himself more competently cruel than his colleagues he started working 'overtime' by carrying out 'patrols' in the field. This brought in more money. He became notorious for ripping open the torsos of his victims and eating their raw hearts. As his reputation was known to all, it was hardly surprising that the prisoners were nervous about the driver's chat with him at the bar. As the car passed All Saints' Cathedral on their left, cool-headed Major Kimumwe whispered to his friends to be alert in making a close study of the area behind the State Research building to assess possible obstacles along the escape route.

26

BACK IN OUR CELL

Time was entirely too short, but quick-witted Mutumba tricked the sentry who was guarding them by asking to use the lavatory on the ground floor. He knew this lavatory had a small glass back window through which he could examine the back of the building. The sentry agreed, escorting him at gunpoint but permitting him privacy in the cubicle. Mutumba was able to study the seven-foot wall which we would have to climb before tackling the fences which were even higher.

Mutumba didn't linger long in the lavatory and was brought back down with the others, to the cell. To show how docile they were, Major Kimumwe suggested they ask the sentries to help them out of their new shirts. The sentries were delighted with this bonus loot. One of them said to him, '*Sasa wewe ndiyo major mzuri*' which translated loosely means, 'You're the right sort of major.'

'Don't worry, chaps,' Kasujja said to us as soon as the sentries had gone, 'we're still alive. But what about our hole? Have you been able to enlarge it further?'

We were all excited at the return of our cell-mates but this question was a bit unfair to those of us who remained behind. If the bars defied the efforts of eight men, how could he have expected them to move at half-strength? 'Don't be silly, Kasujja,' Nambale reprimanded him. 'Do you expect us to do the impossible? In fact, if you hadn't come back we were going to leave you.'

'Gentlemen,' Okech intervened, 'let's simmer down and hear what our friends have been through.'

'We've seen Amin, he has appointed a tribunal to try us. Mr Masikio is the chairman,' Major Kimumwe summarized briefly. It sounded so straightforward that none of us felt the threat of death it was supposed to convey.

'Anyway,' Ssendawula broke the silence, 'we have to work on our ventilator all the harder because we know there's simply no alternative. We'll be lucky to be alive if the tribunal ever takes place – that fellow Simba may show up any minute.'

We sat quietly as our friends told their story. Mr Masikio was Colonel Juma under yet another nickname, this one mostly used in the barracks because of his long flapping ears. Another infamous member of the tribunal was to be Captain Ssebbi. Black and short, his huge body and big belly made him appear even shorter. His waist was non-existent because his stomach touched his thighs. Looking at him sideways, he had no curve from neck to knee because despite his heaviness his buttocks were flat. He, too, was a notorious killer.

We considered the unlikely chance of getting through the tribunal, trying to establish what points in our statements could be used to incriminate us. We concluded that, even if the tribunal exonerated us, our chances of survival were still nil. People had been killed even after courts set them free; we'd be no exception.

That night we again attacked the ventilator bars but failed to budge them. Although the rest of the night was uneventful the following day was harrowing.

Because of the stink of our cells the guards avoided entering them. Whenever food was brought, it was dished out in the open area between the two cells. Ours was given to us in one container at the gate. Plates were collected from the same point. The guards were convinced we couldn't conceivably escape through the concrete walls; all that concerned them was an upstairs escape which is why padlocks were changed daily.

Perhaps God wished to reveal to us His power, or perhaps because of our increasing doubt in Him we'd become so sinful that death was a proper punishment from which He chose to save us. However it's described, we considered it a miracle. When the guard collected our plates around 1.30 p.m. something disturbed him and, for the first time during our imprisonment, he stepped inside the cell asking inconsequential questions about the accumulated dirty shirts, trousers and shoes of those already killed. Most of us were paralysed; we knew he could not fail to see the ventilator and our hole. It was Okech who saved us. On the spur of the moment, Okech blocked his way, standing directly in front of him, face to face. The two were of approximately the same height, weight and size. Okech asked, as always, for cigarettes, 'Efendi, nipatie sigara,' which so enraged the guard that he slapped Okech twice, kicked him once and turned on his heel to march angrily out of the cell.

When he'd disappeared upstairs, we knelt and prayed. We thanked John Okech for having saved us.

27

DISUNITY BETWEEN THE SLIGHTS AND THE HEAVIES

This incident had two results. While all of us were grateful to Okech, the 'slights' now put the blame for the incident on the 'heavies' claiming had it not been for the heavies, most of us would have escaped long ago. They argued that we should escape on an individual basis and it should be an individual decision if anyone remained behind. The heavies wanted the slights to be more grateful because, had it not been for Okech's quick thinking — and he was the heaviest of us and the most hard-working — they as well as the rest of us would have been killed. Furthermore, without the weight and energy of the heavies, the bars couldn't have been bent in the first place.

Although we buried our differences, the gap between the slight group and the heavy group became dangerously pronounced. Teamwork flagged. Nambale invented an excuse for lying down while we were working. Kasujja said his leg hurt him too much to stand on it any more. Even without him as sentry by the gate we worked unsuccessfully on, with Okech expending the most effort. Finally even he got irritated and threatened to make a noise unless everyone got up and worked as before.

Our escape plan met near-disaster that same night as the slights attempted to escape alone. After considerable persuasion it was agreed that the next morning with our combined renewed effort and revived team spirit we would try once again to bend the bars just that necessary bit more.

The next day we were back at work as usual when around 11 a.m. Kasujja called '*Mmese*', repeating this twice so that when the 'rat' approached our cell gate we were where we should be. This was a genuine 'rat', a huge fellow who had come from Bugolobi barracks, and he checked through the gate how many of us there were. When he asked why we were lying down at that hour of the day nobody replied. '*Nani huyo analala?*' he asked, exasperated, 'Who is that one sleeping?' and pointed to Major Kimumwe.

As I was squatting nearest to him, I made the mistake of saying, '*Ndiyo yeye major . . . Efendi,*' meaning 'It's the major, my lord.'

'Major? Major?' he asked, in a temper. 'Who is major? Can a prisoner also be called a major? This is ridiculous.' He requested the gate keys to be brought from upstairs immediately, so that he could teach us a lesson. 'These fellows wanted to kill us and now they call themselves majors!' he fumed as the gate was opened.

We had already agreed that should anybody come into the cell we would confront him in a bunch by the gate. As this 'rat' was intent on beating us up, we formed an arc a few feet from the gate enabling him to go from one end to the other beating each of us. He finished with the end nearest the ventilator and started his second round, this time pulling out hair and moustaches and squeezing genitals. At the end of the second round, still unsatisfied with the amount of pain he'd inflicted on us, he started kicking us – possibly his fingers were sore by now. After kicking three of us, he said he was now going to inspect the cell.

Inspect the cell!

He might as well say 'I will now shoot you.' There was no imaginable way he could miss seeing the hole. We hadn't minded the beating and kicking so long as our ventilator was safe but even the most cursory inspection of our cell must spell our doom.

Perhaps this was another test sent by God, because just as he turned his head towards the ventilator someone came rushing down the stairs as if pursued by devils and shouting, '*Efendi!*'

This disconcerted him. He stood in front of me facing the ventilator and frowning.

'Who is that fool calling *Efendi*?' he demanded, turning around to see him. 'What is it you want?' he snapped as the messenger reached the gate, too much out of breath to speak. 'What's the matter?'

'*Efendi*, you are wanted upstairs,' the messenger said, still panting.

'Who is it who wants me there?'

'*Efendi*, the boss wants you most urgently,' the messenger replied.

Grudgingly the officer accepted the request, saying, 'Let me give these prisoners a final round before I come.'

We were hardly aware of the final round, in fact it rather woke all of us from the paralysed trance we'd gone into. After his departure we gathered together and prayed. It was too much to believe that an officer able to see our hole would not recognize what it signified merely because he was distracted by a messenger. The miracle increased our disunity because the slights made it crystal clear they had no intention of waiting for further close shaves and miracle rescues.

'Should we all die here just because of one fat fellow who couldn't control his diet?' they asked. Nobody answered. Later on there was some frank but aimless discussion. Much later we learned we'd been saved by the mistake made by the Bugolobi major in coming downstairs without permission of Minawa who was in his office at the time. Minawa took it as unforgivably rude for an outsider, no matter of what rank, to inspect this station without even paying him a courtesy call and so sent for him in a great hurry simply to establish his authority. Another mistake the visitor unwittingly made was in beating up the 'presidential prisoners' without Minawa's knowledge or consent.

In a final compromise it was agreed we make a last attempt to widen the hole and escape that very night. We started work and at around 4.30 p.m. we hoped we had now bent the bar sufficiently for Okech to get through. We still attempted to dig

124

around it with spoons and metal oddments in an effort to pull it out completely.

When the time came, we removed our handcuffs, opened up the ventilator, lifted Okech and pushed him through the hole, head first. Okech was heavy and, although he was a soldier, he lacked agility. We pushed hard for almost ten minutes but his chest could not go through. He began breathing stentoriously so we pulled him back. This was the most frustrating and difficult part of our exercise before our actual escape. We'd postponed our 'departure' to accommodate Okech and still Okech couldn't get through. What next?

The slights group demanded we escape and leave Okech behind. 'After all,' one of them said, 'we're not responsible for his bigness. If he couldn't control his weight, that's his problem, everybody should learn to eat properly and keep their weight down.'

'But don't you know that without my weight applied to it that heavy bar wouldn't have bent at all?' Okech retorted.

It was still the case that we fell into three categories: slights, mediums and heavies. Nambale announced he would defy any resolution other than one endorsing immediate escape. Okech counteracted this by stating that if anybody escaped, he'd raise an alarm which would result in everybody's death. 'After all,' he pointed out, 'it's you who drafted me into this.'

In the ensuing deadlock we drifted to our sleeping areas and half an hour later Major Kimumwe went round canvassing for just one more unwanted and unpopular postponement. 'Please, only one more and then absolutely no more,' he cajoled Mutumba who was stretched full length next to me.

'W-e-l-l,' Mutumba said thoughtfully, 'personally, I'm willing to give Okech one more chance but that's absolutely all.'

Kimumwe skipped me – he knew what I'd say – and went to Nambale in the same row at the far end. 'Mr Nambale, I know your feelings,' he began, 'but you're a man. Can't you risk your life for one more day only for our sakes? Everybody else has agreed to do so. Why do you want to be different? Remember what

125

we've been saying all along, that we should all leave together. Can you imagine what would happen if it were you and not Okech?'

'Let's stay just one more night.' Mutumba added his support to Kimumwe's but Nambale turned his face away. This at least seemed to indicate he no longer insisted on escaping alone. Kimumwe then called us together to formalize the postponement. He ended by saying, 'Tomorrow is the last day.'

28

TOMORROW IS THE LAST DAY

'Tomorrow is the last day, come what may.'

'Tomorrow I'm not staying here,' Nambale mumbled.

'I, too, am not sleeping here,' Mutumba added. 'Even if it means leaving everybody here, I'll do so. You guys have been postponing our escape too often, that's why even God wants to punish you. He showed you the way, yet you've refused to take it. OK chaps, I don't want to die here like a dumb animal. Tomorrow I'm off. I'll sleep here no more. F-u-l-l s-t-o-p.'

Everybody endorsed this statement except Okech, who looked dissatisfied and muttered something about 'being pushed into it too fast'. He was still muttering when we retired to our sleeping places.

Friday, 23 September was an important day for us, it was the unforgettable day we were determined to taste again the air of freedom. We awakened early to work on our last push. Usually we started at 9 a.m. when the hubbub of office workers was on, but because of the ultimatum given us by the slights group we began work on the bar around 7 a.m., a move which almost cost us our lives.

I was on the listening watch by the other ventilator and Kasujja was at the gate. The work was progressing smoothly when suddenly I saw someone between the louvres. He was wearing a pair of long pink trousers and platform shoes. As he faced away from the building, all I could see were his heels.

Immediately, I signalled my friends to stop work but because the warning usually meant 'rats' were coming down the stairs it took them a few seconds to understand what was wrong. I signalled more urgently and whispered '*Mmese*'. There was panic.

The fellow was standing almost by the ventilator and there was no reason to doubt that he was listening to our noise. The projector stand was pulled down and Ssekalo poked his hand through the hole to pull the wire gauze into position. This was risky because he so easily could have touched the fellow, but it had to be done to conceal the hole. Some of my friends came to peep through the louvres to satisfy their curiosity.

The fellow still stood there, statue-like. We quickly closed up the hole, hurriedly hung up a shirt, then knelt and prayed, fully expecting the rattling of machine-gun fire into our cell. We prayed for about half an hour, Major Kimumwe preaching from the New Testament about Jesus saving the disciples drowning in the lake. We didn't pay much attention to the lesson, our minds were halfway between God and death. Half an hour was very much longer than usual and, considering the impatience of the State Research Bureau boys, we began to hope that the fellow had somehow unbelievably not heard our noise. We dared to rejoice a bit, knelt again and thanked God for having kept that fellow deaf. It was impossible that a normal person on patrol could fail to hear excessive sound just below his heels. The ventilators had slanting concrete covers or shades which made it difficult for someone outside to see the louvres without deliberately bending down. Resuming work after this shock took some time but we had to get going because of our own ultimatum. Around 11 a.m. it was apparent the movement of the bars had increased the size of the hole enough to let Okech through. We stopped and prepared for countdown.

Okech was doubtful so it was suggested that we measure the diameter of the hole yet again and compare it with Okech's chest. The results were quite good and everybody seemed reasonably content. The guard brought us lunch as usual, which was added proof that nobody had heard us work. We were too keyed up to eat and for the first time food was taken back. After lunch we played draughts until 5 p.m. when Okech expressed his nagging uneasiness. 'Gentlemen,' he said, 'suppose I fail to go through?'

Nobody replied. All of us knew there was no alternative but death. We had all accepted the ultimatum and everybody except Okech was thoroughly fed up with the frequent shocks that followed our repeated postponements.

'Suppose I do not go through?' Okech repeated. 'I'm not entirely convinced I will go through.' He moved to the ventilator, looked at it intently as if asking it to reply to his query, turned around and asked Kimumwe, 'Do you really think I'll get through that hole?'

'I think you will,' Kimumwe replied.

'But suppose I don't?' Okech pressed.

'I'm sure you will,' Kimumwe repeated reassuringly.

Okech picked up a piece of string and measured the diameter of the hole yet again then asked me to arrange two boxes for him to wriggle between while one of us sat on each.

'You see!' Mutumba exclaimed triumphantly. 'You'll go through. You don't have to worry about the alternatives.'

But now I began to have my doubts. I crossed to where Kimumwe lay and asked him in a low voice if he were really convinced Okech could go through. To my embarrassment, he pushed me aside with the statement that of course Okech would go through. 'But what will happen if he doesn't?' I persisted. My question was unwelcome. Even Kimumwe had made up his mind to go, no matter who was left behind. I moved to Ssendawula and appealed to him to try to plan for an alternative. He was unhelpful.

For the first time since captivity we were all now behaving as individuals. The general attitude was that now everybody should look after himself.

Okech paced around the cell for some minutes then stopped at the ventilator. He tried to pull out the bent bar but it merely rotated in its socket. 'Is it really impossible for us to pull out this rotating bar?' he asked.

Nobody bothered to reply. There was one accepted topic of general interest – the route each was to take after overcoming the

129

immediate obstacles. It was decided if we were caught we should not disclose the position or route of our friends, regardless of what torture was applied. If we all got outside the fences safely, everyone, including Kasujja, was to be on his own. We went over each other's possible route. Ssendawula and I were planning to follow the same route. Kasujja changed his route to come with us for possible assistance but later Ssendawula influenced me to turn him down. This was not good, we were being unsympathetic to crippled Kasujja, so we rationalized an excuse. 'Mr Kasujja, I'm sorry, we won't be able to go together as planned because I'm taking a different route,' Ssendawula told him.

'OK,' Kasujja said thoughtfully. 'I know you've done so because you think I'll be a burden. I'll be able to make it on my own.'

Much later, over drinks in Nairobi, Kasujja recalled this incident to our acute embarrassment.

29

THE LAST NIGHT – EXECUTIONS DELAY OUR ESCAPE

Since the meeting with Amin in his Cape Town Villa, we'd noticed a change in the security organization at Nakasero. Not only were the soldiers stricter but many more were on night duty, with increased night patrols at the back of the building – but fortunately these were regular, taking place at even hours.

Soldiers were always on the ground floor, but that particular night we were surprised to see a large number flocking downstairs at about 8 p.m. This worried us. They walked aimlessly up and down for an hour or so which made some of us curse Okech for having delayed us.

To crown it all there was an ugly fat soldier, bare-chested and wearing only shorts, who held a rifle with several magazines on his shoulder and who carried a *panga*, or machete. Although he walked lazily, he took an obvious and keen interest in the prisoners in Cell 1. After ambling around the corridor between the two cells he began sharpening his machete on the floor, talking to himself in a half-crazed manner. Possibly he'd been smoking *bhang* (African cannabis) and was intoxicated. Normally soldiers cultivated such a condition before the execution exercises, which gave us an indication of what might be about to take place. We could understand nothing of his unintelligible mumbling. We finally made out one statement which he addressed repeatedly to those in Cell I. '*Hi itakula nyinyi leo,*' which in Swahili meant, 'This will cut you tonight.'

After he'd taken himself upstairs, we heard all the soldiers assembling as for a parade and someone was giving them instructions. We heard a loud telephone call and then cars arrived at the prison. We noted one in particular, the sergeant's because of its spectacular noise. It was an ancient Austin Cambridge which he often used for bringing us food. Immediately after the last car entered, the execution exercise started. The diesel generator was switched on and one by one the prisoners were killed on the ground floor. There were screams, cries, last-minute entreaties for mercy, all in vain. It appeared as though that night the executions were of civil servants, particularly from the Ministry of Culture.

For some unknown reason, Amin had turned against the actors and organizers of a play called *Oluyimba Lwa Wankoko* staged by Uganda in Lagos (Nigeria) at the All-African Drama Festival. Amin had seen and approved of the play before the troupe left for Lagos, as it was much too risky to stage it without his approval and the green light from the State Research Bureau.

Despite these precautions, however, Amin was told — and believed — the play subtly depicted him as a dictator and murderer. He promptly condemned everyone from the Ministry of Culture and for those who had taken part in, or organized the play the punishment was death. The last man to be killed that night was a man called Mukasa, no relation to Galabuzi Mukasa whose watch we were using.

Both of them were Baganda, Christians and employees of the Ministry of Culture. Galabuzi Mukasa had also been connected with the play; possibly that's why he'd been put in Cell 2 while the other Mukasa, who was just a clerk, was locked up in Cell 1. Galabuzi Mukasa had been killed some time ago and had it not been for his automatic watch and tweed jacket would no longer be remembered.

'Mukasa, Mukasa, Mukasa!' one of the soldiers had called, coming downstairs. Nobody answered. A few minutes later another soldier had come down, a Nubian fluent in Luganda. 'Mr

Mukasa, please come out,' he ordered, opening the door of Cell 1. 'Don't be afraid,' he said and added in Luganda, '*Totya*', which means the same. He patted Mukasa's shoulders to reassure him. That was the last we saw of Mukasa. When we heard a body fall into the lorry outside we realized he, too, had been killed. This was one of my most frightening moments in Nakasero. According to my rapid calculation, I should logically be in the next lot to face execution.

'Let's escape now, please,' I urged my friends who were calmer than I.

'Cool down,' Major Kimumwe advised, 'this is quite normal. Even in ordinary military life you see people die. Keep calm but be alert. We'll go but let's study the situation.'

'What do you mean? How can we go on when the soldiers are killing everyone around us?'

'Remember, we're special,' Mutumba reminded me. 'Nobody can kill us without President Amin's personal authorization, that's why he's sending us to the tribunal. I'm sure we'll live at least until then.'

'But even people like Mr Foreign Exchange and Bob Astles can order us killed provided they notify him,' Kimumwe said. Mr Foreign Exchange was the popular name for Adirisi Mustafa, the current vice-president, an illiterate. He had threatened to shoot dead 'Mr Foreign Exchange' at the Bank of Uganda because of his persistent absence from the bank when everyone was looking for him. It was told of him that one day when he was particularly disgruntled at the 'lack of foreign exchange reports', he marched to the Bank of Uganda prepared to arrest and put to instant death this irresponsible servant who was always leaving his office to attend to private business. '*Wapi yeye?*' he asked in a temper. 'Where is he?' '*Mimi nataka ua yeye. Anafikiri ye ni nani? Kama sisi tunaweza shika Mkuu wa sheria, yeye ni nani?*' Who was that Foreign Exchange person and just how important did he consider himself? Certainly not more important than Chief Justice Kiwanuka (who had been arrested and killed)!

The other VIP in the regime was an Englishman, Bob Astles, who had lived in Uganda for a long time before the country became independent. According to available records he was like the majority of white people in former British colonies. He obtained employment in the Ministry of Works not because of his professional qualifications but because of his colour. Being white, he quickly rose to the rank of foreman. He had a unique ability to win favours, and through this talent he switched effortlessly and smoothly from one regime to another. He won the confidence of Uganda's first independent government, which gave him several undeserved promotions. It is claimed he was instrumental in the detention of five cabinet ministers who were arrested by President Obote in 1966. When Amin overthrew Obote, Bob Astles was on hand to give the new president advice on all British affairs. At one time he narrowly escaped a trap set by his African colleagues (Amin's thugs) who wanted to kill him for misreporting them to Amin. He escaped across the lake in a canoe to the Kenyan town of Kisumu on Lake Victoria. From Kenya he flew to London, where he engaged in pro-Amin propaganda on the BBC, both over radio and on television.

The favourable propaganda so moved Amin that he appealed to Astles to return home and, to the disgust of most Africans, Astles returned to a position of exceptional strength and power. He was promoted to the rank of major and placed in charge of the anti-smuggling squad. He was of medium build, and sported a moustache which, with his piercing blue eyes, made him appear formidable. His Muganda wife, Mary Senkatuuka of a famous Baganda family, was appointed a minister of culture by Amin because of her husband's influence. To attain his objectives, Astles renounced his British citizenship. Many considered him a double-dealer, working for Amin while at the same time on the payroll of several international spy syndicates. Others rated him as dangerous as Amin himself. Whatever he said nobody dared challenge him.

From our talk, I realized we could be killed only when one of the three VIPs ordered our death. 'But suppose the order has already been given? How would we know?' I asked. I argued that we should escape while there was so much noise on the ground floor and the sentries' attention was focused on the killings, but my friends flatly refused.

When the killings stopped we sighed in relief, knowing we'd been spared for one more night, the most important night of all. A guard came downstairs to check on us, asking Major Kimumwe whether we were all accounted for and accepting his affirmative reply. He switched off the lights and left. Ten minutes later two sentries brought us tit-bits, sweets and bananas, but as they were about to leave, Kasujja, nearest the entrance, shouted to them to bring us cigarettes. This was an indirect way of asking them not to come back, but these sentries behaved differently from the norm. They brought us several packets of Sportsman cigarettes. After their departure another sentry brought us almost immediately ten well-cooked chapatis, big pancakes. The sentry was a Nubian guard who knew Patrick Kimumwe from Malire barracks, and could have been a close relative of Vice-President Mustafa Adirisi. After an amiable chat with Patrick, he left politely wishing us good-night. Kimumwe told us about him, saying his name was 'Pending' because of his constant misuse of the word.

Although my friends ate the chapatis, I was far too nervous to swallow anything. It was suggested we have a prayer session as we felt God had already blessed our escape by showing us kindness through the actions of the sentries. The prayers were short and we took up our assigned watching places, two by the ventilator and Kasujja by the gate making movements as if he had to go to the toilet. We counted the cars as they left; the sergeant's was the last to go, at midnight.

30

ZERO HOUR – WE SHALL
LEAVE TONIGHT

'You see, Mr Kato,' Kimumwe whispered to me, 'as I told you, we shall leave tonight. All we need do now is be extra-careful.'

We couldn't sleep or even cat-nap because of the tension. We used all our senses to their maximum. We listened with our sixteen ears pushing our hearing beyond all limits reached before. Half of us concentrated on sounds in the State Research building and the rest on the grounds outside. Quiet reigned inside the building; the last noises were from the guards preparing their sleeping places on the ground floor as others walked to theirs on the upper floors. It was uncannily quiet, yet we sensed something was taking place outside as we could hear raised voices. We concentrated and finally located the disturbance at the main entrance gate.

The voices belonged to the still alert quarter guards. This was most unwelcome as the guards were only a few metres away from our ventilators at the very spot where we planned to leave the cell. This meant we must revise our plans. Although we'd decided against using the underground drainage pipes we hadn't completely discarded the idea. One of our surveys had shown us that the drainage trench that ran along the building was deep enough to conceal us from the sentries once we got out. We decided to use the trench only for immediate hiding, if necessary, and to be extremely cautious. We also had to be careful not to alert anyone in the adjoining cell. We heard the noise coming from a night-club some distance away and dogs barked incessantly. Zero hour had always been 1 a.m. because then the sentries had finished their midnight patrol and wouldn't do their rounds again until 2 a.m. It was the period of deepest sleep for the guards.

Exactly at 1 a.m. we sat in a semi-circle and prayed to God to bless our escape. We comforted each other, saying, 'There is no death which is good or bad. All human beings come to the same end. It is better we die of gunshots while climbing fences to freedom than die of similar shots while tied to a tree or an empty petrol drum. The whole world will know and sympathize with us. And if we die escaping from our cell, this will be another victory for our cause.'

We prayed for courage and protection and then Kimumwe said, 'Before we say the grace of Our Lord together, I appeal to God to let us go, whether for good, life or death, now and in His name.'

All of us replied 'Amen'.

31

OKECH WON'T GO THROUGH

Okech spoke. 'Let us *all* go in the name of Our Lord Jesus Christ, let us go.'

On opening the hole we found there was too much moonlight and we decided it would be prudent to wait another half-hour and then make the final attempt; we couldn't wisely postpone it until 3 a.m. We made final checks, took off our handcuffs, locked them again and each one placed his pair at the foot of his sleeping place. Then we opened up the hole and lifted our friend Okech into it, head first. We pushed and pushed but Okech could not go through. We tried several ways, including legs instead of head first but with no success. There was a suggestion to let Ssekalo out first so that he could pull Okech from outside but we feared that in case of failure Ssekalo would never come back.

We finally gave up and stood despondently by the ventilator. 'I told you,' Okech broke the silence, 'I told you gentlemen that I wouldn't go through but you insisted I would. Now what do we do?'

'Now what do we do?' Nambale repeated. 'We're going.'

'Going?' Okech asked, outraged. 'If you go I'll make sure you get shot just outside!'

'So what *do* we do now?' Kasujja asked.

It was past 2 a.m. but we were prepared to risk confronting the guards on patrol. I proposed we try again. We lifted Okech back into the hole and pushed him as hard as we could, but he was just too fat. We helped him down, knowing there was no way he would ever get through that ventilator. None of us had any illusions about what this meant. The State Research thugs would never let the only caged bird live when the others had flown to freedom with his help.

'Gentlemen, I told you to endeavour to pull out the rotating bar, but you refused. We must wait and do that tomorrow morning. I am not going to let you go alone. We must stick to our earlier decision. We must escape or die together. Nothing more,' Okech said firmly.

We were now in a hopeless dilemma. According to our ultimatum we had to leave, but this new problem was unforeseen. What made the situation so blatantly unjust was that Okech had exerted by far the most strength and without him we would never have reached this stage. There was a moral obligation to heed his appeal. It was now 2.30 a.m. We sat down and pleaded with him, but in vain. Nambale and Mutumba, disgusted with everything, moved to their places and lay down, Nambale on his back staring at the ceiling, Mutumba with his face buried in his arms. I moved over to Okech and asked him to listen to me, as to an older brother, with an open mind. He agreed, but said he wanted to explain his position.

He had been arrested because of his friend Ssendawula who was now leaving him to die alone. While he had been taking an evening walk in Entebbe Town, Ssendawula stopped his car and asked Okech to accompany him to Baita-Ababiri, two miles along the Entebbe–Kampala road, to buy liver for his wife who was in hospital. On their way back they were flagged down by State Research boys, but Ssendawula refused to stop. The boys followed them to the Katabi (Entebbe) barracks where the two were arrested.

I assured him of my appreciation of his case but again appealed to him to save our lives. 'I know it's difficult for you to understand our position,' I said. 'I don't think you'll be killed because you're so patently innocent. Remember how I was prepared to die and let you escape? You must be a good statesman.'

'But does that mean that I, who have worked the hardest of all, am the one to be left behind? No, not me, we must die together,' he insisted.

I explained further. His innocence was known even by the commander of the marines who would ensure he was pardoned. All he needed was to invent a good explanation dissociating himself from our plan. I reminded him of our earlier suggestion of either pretending he was fast asleep when we escaped or that we'd been let out by unknown soldiers or guards who'd refused to let him escape, too.

After a good deal of thought he took a deep breath and, deeply disappointed and bitterly hurt, he reluctantly said, 'OK. Try your luck, but please remember I am going to die for you. You should feel obliged to try to secure my release, and if that fails you should support my family.'

This was all we needed. It was Okech's 'OK' we'd been waiting for. Nambale and Mutumba jumped from their places, Mutumba danced and Nambale said, 'Now Mr Okech, you have shown the sort of noble and mature person you are. We owe our lives to you.'

We all thanked him and then resumed our escape work hurriedly. As we lifted the first person to the hole, Okech began to sob but, being a great and brave person, pulled himself together and said that the first thing he wanted us to do was to advise his wife and mother of the dangerous situation in which we were leaving him. He then agreed to our request that he would wait at least two hours before making any noise. This was needed for us to gain distance and outwit the State Research Bureau boys in their search for us.

Okech was killed by Amin's thugs. May Almighty God let him rest in peace. We owe our lives to him. We would like to pay tribute to him for having sacrificed his life for us.

32

WRIGGLING OUT OF THE DEATH TRAP

It was 3 a.m. when we lifted Ssekalo, the second fattest, up to the bars. He was instructed to make a quick check as soon as he was out and signal to us appropriately. Ssekalo struggled hard to go through and did exactly what the dove did when it was sent from Noah's ark. Soon he gave us the 'thumbs up' signal that all was well. Excitement took over and everyone wanted to be the next to leave. However, Kimumwe had obviously to be next, and he was followed by Ssendawula. Fourth was Kasujja and I was fifth. Going through was not at all easy, even for a man of my medium size. First you lifted yourself off the floor by holding and pulling on the two bars. A friend then lifted your body up to bring it to the level of the ventilator. This enabled the right arm and then the head to be pushed through. Then, by twisting to one side, you could get your shoulders to go through vertically. Even at that point you were dependent on the force of your friends because you had only one hand to pull yourself out. With the chest through and with the use of both hands on the ground – this was ground level – pulling the hips through was relatively easy. When you were outside, you signalled the next fellow to come and also to give you your clothes because you had to go through naked, or with underwear only, if you still had any.

Nambale followed me and Mutumba was the last, helped by Okech to whom he bade a sad farewell. 'Good luck, John,' we whispered to Okech who, in turn, wished us the same saying, 'Good luck, goodbye, you go well, let me die for you.'

Both sides needed the luck: Okech was at the mercy of Amin's thugs; we were in God's hands.

What a change! The air of freedom was heady but the fear of gunshots made some of us tremble. After putting on our clothes, each of us took place in a row, squatting down in the drainage trench and figuring out what to do next. We felt as if we'd just risen from the dead. We were in a new world. Our grave down below was still fresh and the heavens above full of glory but the question 'What to do next?' required an immediate answer.

The air was cool and the sky bright with moonlight and stars. The night was still silent except for the barking of the dogs in the house next to where we were. This was the sort of atmosphere one would like for an outing, along the beach or in the countryside, or on a holiday. Had it not been for the mental torment of our situation, one would have wanted to recall the soft nights of one's honeymoon.

Ssekalo had done a good job when he whispered to us, 'The State Research quarter guards are only a few feet north of us.' We could see them. Their voices were loud and clear but we had little interest in their conversation. It had been agreed that once outside the cell there would be no talking, save for an emergency, only signs would be used. We had to follow the command of Major Kimumwe like soldiers, without questioning. We were a little higher than the quarter guards on the northern side so we crawled to the south along the western side of the building until we came to the end of the building where, for the first time, we were obliged to come into a lighted sector.

We stopped and squatted while Ssekalo peered across to see if all was clear. The light came from the front of the building. Fortunately not a single soldier was about. We crossed from the corner tip of the building to the seven-foot wall which Mutumba had warned us of. We had to climb it in order to reach the level where we could tackle the fences. Because the building was on the slopes of Nakasero hill, the upper side of the ground was quite high and a concrete wall encircled all of it. There was no other way, except the suicidal one of passing in front of the building. We quickly lifted Ssekalo to the top of the wall; he pulled up Kimumwe, who in turn pulled up Kasujja as we pushed from below. The rest of us went up fairly easily.

We were now close to the first perimeter fence which was brightly lit by security lights all around save at the rear. It was definitely possible to be seen by the guards on stand-by in vehicles at the front of the building, therefore we had to find a darker place to go through, over or under the fence, which meant moving west. We tackled the slope slowly at a westerly angle, encountering one place where the barbed wire was not too tight. We climbed the fence which tested our ability and wits and was a miracle of manoeuvring for the crippled Kasujja.

Now we faced a much stronger fence which we feared might be electrified. Kimumwe signalled us to sit down while Ssekalo selected the next most suitable place to go through. This was not easy to find. Ssekalo reported that a possible spot was at the northern end. This necessitated climbing down the slope and over the fence and into the grounds of the neighbouring house. Apart from the climbing, there were two major problems along this route: the place was too near the quarter guards and there were two ferocious dogs in the neighbour's compound who had been barking ever since we emerged from our cell.

Kasujja suggested two of us climb the fence and from the top of it jump on the dogs and strangle them while two more of us came to their assistance immediately. This sounded feasible, but what about the noise the protesting and powerful dogs would make? Wouldn't such a commotion alert both the owner and the quarter guards? The idea was dropped but before we found an alternative and while Ssekalo was still debating where to go next, a soldier came around the southern corner of the building, possibly on patrol. He walked towards the ventilator but stopped ten metres from it. He carried a rifle. We watched him turn around and go back to the front of the building, a small incident but one which shocked us profoundly. Our hearts hammered with the realization we were still in grave danger.

Kimumwe signalled to Ssekalo to make another survey with

particular emphasis on the bottom of the fence. We saw him kneel and attempt to lift the fence where a depression had been prepared to drain water. The fence was deliberately loosened for about a foot and a half. We decided to get under there, profoundly relieved that the fence was not, after all, electrified. We wriggled through with our heads sideways, then turned around to face the sky and, lying on our backs, dragged our bodies through. We were pleased with our progress; so far so good. We were now outside the prison fencing, although still surrounded by more wire. The only way out seemed to be through the French ambassador's residence but this was to the east of the prison and reaching it necessitated going around the front of the building.

Assuming his rightful position, Major Kimumwe led us crawling, heads down, up the corridor with the intention of going around the front courtyard of the State Research building. The corridor was well lit by security lighting, but we were relying on the creeping plants that had grown on the prison side of the fence to give us protective covering.

Ssendawula followed Kimumwe, and I was third. It was nerveracking but we had no other choice. Three of us were directly in line with the entrance to the reception when Kimumwe signalled us to halt. We were now all in full bright light and looking down we could see, some ten feet below on our left, seated soldiers, some on the pavement, others on the verandah and some inside vehicles. One or two stood, holding rifles on their shoulders. We were sure we must be seen and expected bullets to finish us off.

Things had definitely gone wrong; we had made a serious mistake in taking this route. The sight of the soldiers so near terrified us. We retreated to the dark area where we sighed in relief. God was with us, He had saved us again. We collected under a tree to decide our next move but the dry crackling of leaves made our movements noisy. While we considered what to do, Ssekalo made yet another reconnaissance, but by now the dogs were barking so frantically he was afraid to touch the fence. Only a fool of a security guard could have failed to check on those dogs, a spot of luck for us once again.

We had left Okech with the watch and could not tell the exact time, but it must have been around 4 a.m. when someone switched on a light in the building and suddenly we were all exposed. Kimumwe immediately ordered us to lie flat but again the dry leaves made a dreadful rustling. When I started to raise my head to see who had turned on the light Kasujja, using one leg, kicked me hard. I learned later that a female officer had walked to the toilet on the first floor and when she had switched on the light it streamed through the open window and fell on us. Almost simultaneously light came from the window of the adjacent toilet to illuminate our spot even more. I saw who did it this time: a soldier in uniform carrying a rifle. After easing himself, he had a drink of water then switched off the light and left while the woman was busily beautifying herself before the mirror. After applying lipstick to her satisfaction, she left, turning off the light.

During this episode we had frozen, holding our breath, immobile. In darkness again, we vigorously searched for an alternative route. I discovered a gap in the fence leading to the servants' quarters of the Presidential Lodge but while I was still widening it — it was only six inches in diameter — Nambale and Mutumba discovered a bigger one, probably used by houseboys and their girlfriends. We were uncertain where the latter led, so we decided to widen mine, which we used. Luckily there were no dogs in the Presidential Lodge grounds and everyone was asleep in the servants' quarters. Aided by darkness we walked past the quarters on the concrete path leading to the main entrance. Nambale and myself walked confidently, prepared to pretend we were occupants, while the others hid among the bamboo trees along the path. If accosted, we could say we were going out for a purpose, claiming to be servants of the Presidential Lodge.

Normally the gate and the area would be guarded by military police, commonly known as 'Red Tops', but we found it unattended and, as a group, decided to modify our route to avoid the danger of going through the main entrance. Slipping through a fence on our immediate right we found ourselves near a building known as the 'annexe' to the lodge. This area was too brightly lit to appeal to us although everything was quiet. There was no sign of Okech's having raised any alarm. As far as we could see there was only one more fence to clear before reaching safety. Two gates, one to the lodge itself, the other to the annexe, were only a few metres apart. This meant that to pass through the annexe gate we must risk being seen or shot at by the military police guards at the main entrance. The annexe gate presented no problem, it was short, but how to reach it was ticklish. There was no barrier between us and the tempting gate but the entire area was brilliantly illuminated.

By this time discipline had become low because we were nearing freedom and nobody wanted to risk being caught. We crossed from one tree shadow to the next until we reached the last shadow before the gate. Here we became aware that the gate did not close flush with the ground. There was a big gap at one end which made us abandon any plan to climb it, preferring to pass underneath it on our backs. Having done so we were free and the whole world seemed to belong to us. We felt great.

From the gate we reached the public road leading from All Saints' Cathedral to the Presidential Lodge. The sole disturbance came from the dogs still barking at us from nearby houses. Otherwise each of us, Kasujja included, walked as if he was going to heaven having left hell behind. Kasujja had picked up a stick and was walking upright and fast. We hurried as much as we could but, as we were barefoot, it was painful treading on the pointed loose stones on the road.

The All Saints' Cathedral road junction was our dispersal point. Each of us would then be on his own with no responsibility towards the others. Kimumwe and Mutumba stuck together. By the grace of God we all seven made it to Nairobi, in neighbouring Kenya.

33

EVERYBODY GOES HIS OWN WAY

When we met again we each had a different and equally compelling story to tell.

One of us went round the southern part of Lake Victoria via Masaka, Mutukula, Bukoba, Mwanza and Kisumu. Somewhere between Bukoba and Mwanza he was arrested by 'Ugandan rebels' who were planning to invade Uganda. They suspected him of being Amin's spy and handed him over to the Tanzanian authorities who, after a thorough interrogation, released him but ordered him to leave the country at once. With assistance, he managed to cross into Kenya and get to Nairobi.

Another went north, crossed Lake Kioga in a canoe, then hiked over the Sebei Hills into Kenya. He reached Nairobi, via Kitale, after a month.

Poor Kasujja initially had it rough but was later helped by friends who drove him across the Kenya/Uganda border at Busia. When he left us at the junction he found he was unable to walk far with his improvised crutch, so went down on all threes and crawled some distance, the sharp stones forcing him to pause often to rest. Just before dawn he made it to a house he thought he recognized from former times, and because he was desperate, right or wrong he had to get inside. The gate was closed but not locked so that he could open it and hop in, and although he met the inevitable barking dog it wasn't sufficiently fierce to bite

147

him. He knocked at the main door of the house but met with no reply, so he went round to the servants' quarters to hide there until daybreak when he hoped to find somebody familiar. Although the owner had seen him, it wasn't prudent at that time to open one's door to strangers.

After the sun had risen he returned to the main house, which he was now sure belonged to his brother-in-law, and started whispering at the door. The wife recognized Kasujja's voice and asked her husband to open the door. 'That's my brother, Majwala Kasujja, please open the door, I know his voice. He's one of our step-brothers. We'd heard he'd been killed, how come I can hear his voice?'

Her husband was also puzzled. How could a dead man be alive again? The Kasujja he'd known had had two legs, who was this one-legged man? Afraid to open the door to robbers, he cried out, 'Kasujja, Kasujja! It it you? Are you the one?'

'Yes, I am,' Kasujja replied delightedly and, as the door opened, he introduced himself formally. 'Mr Makumbi, I'm your brother-in-law.' There was much rejoicing because, to them, Kasujja had virtually risen from the dead. He briefly told them our story and asked for protection.

'Protection?' Makumbi knew this was highly dangerous; Amin's men could wipe out the whole village if they found out. What could he do with this stupid brother-in-law who brought death into his house? If he refused to protect him, it would look bad to his wife and her relatives. Confused, he invited Kasujja to have a bath, which he certainly needed, while his wife prepared something to eat. This gave him time to think.

He made a few telephone calls but no one answered. He worried that his line had been cut, and walked to the kitchen to consult his wife who said, 'But, darling, we have to protect him.'

Makumbi was now more annoyed than confused, and assured himself he'd married a stupid woman. Back in the living room he sat down at the table to think just as Kasujja emerged from the bathroom, rather too soon for him. Even the food was ready before the couple had decided what to do. Perceptive Kasujja realized, even before eating (and he was hungry), that both his step-sister and her husband were perturbed by his presence. He gave them a lead.

'Dear brother, don't worry so much. I'm not here to stay. I don't want you killed by Amin. Would you try to get in touch with my friend Sam who'll arrange for my transport and further protection?'

The couple were understandably relieved, the husband going to the bedroom to try again on the telephone, the wife asking questions about Kasujja's escape. Life returned to normal. When the husband came back to say Sam was on his way, everyone relaxed and became convivial. Kasujja was locked in the servants' quarters to await Sam's arrival half an hour later and then, after being hidden in several places, was driven to the Kenya/Uganda border with the assistance of a high-ranking army officer.

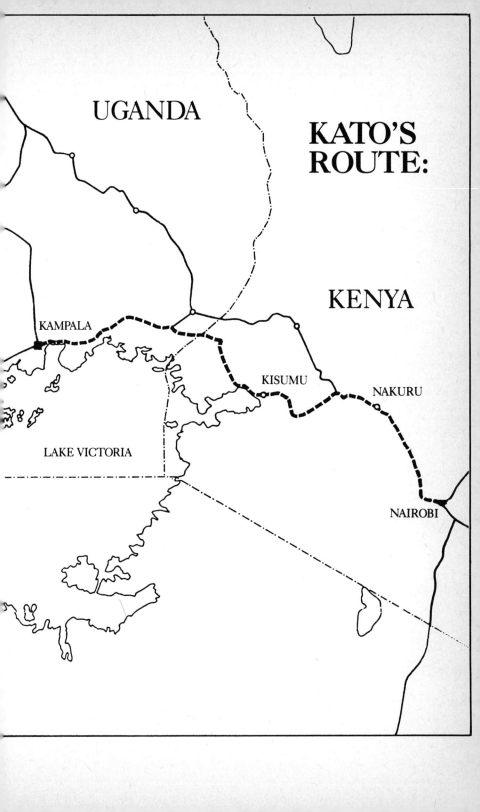

PART THREE

GOAL ATTAINED

34

WALKING TO NAIROBI, A HERCULEAN TASK

My own escape was unmitigated hell; a time came when I'd even wished I'd been shot and killed in the cell rather than endure further misery. From the annexe gate Ssendawula and I hurriedly walked away as planned and, on reaching the road junction, we looked to the right and saw the sentries' hut at the main entrance of the prison. We paused for a few minutes to assess whether there was any sign of movement in the prison as, unlike the rest of our friends, we were to cross the well-lit junction. We were afraid this might arouse the sentries' attention and prompt a check of the cell.

It still seemed quiet, so we plucked up our courage and crossed, going downhill, leaving the cathedral on our left and the prison on our right. Down below we joined a road and increased our speed, but not conspicuously, as we had no wish to alert the nightwatchmen guarding houses along the road. We passed the Fairway Hotel, left the golf club on our right, then started running across the golf course. Ssendawula was tired, and we slowed to a walk for a bit but, realizing we had to gain distance before dawn, I insisted we resume running.

We lost our way and found ourselves in a marsh where two streams crossed. We lost our sense of direction. We had wanted to traverse the golf links and climb the hill to the other side to join the road where I would turn right to walk on until I reached the Jinja road to Nairobi. Ssendawula was to turn left and walk to the nearest suburb, where he hoped to find a friend he'd known a long time ago.

We ran up the hill, but Ssendawula started panting and pleaded with me to slow down. Nearing the top we again lost our way and descended, only to find ourselves near the roundabout along the Kitante road, which meant we'd done a full circle to where we'd crossed into the golf course. This was distressing after all the futile expenditure of energy. Obviously it would be foolish to follow the road, yet it was inadvisable to tackle the marsh again.

We agreed to part.

I went back on to the golf course, but parallel to the Kitante road, until I left the golf club behind, then I turned left and headed east towards Jinja where I would be safe, free and among friends.

My home and family were on the southern side of Kampala and to reach them I would have had to cross the town. I didn't want to do this. Not only would it be risky to walk that distance at night, but my home would be the obvious place to search for me. Having come from Nairobi, where I'd worked for fifteen years, I was tempted to walk the 450-mile distance to save my life without endangering anybody else's.

I set off knowing full well the difficulties involved and the Herculean task it was, but determined to do it. Most likely Okech had given us the agreed time lapse of two hours before raising the alarm, but because we'd squandered more than half of it around the prison itself, none of us had travelled far before hearing the State Research vehicles zooming aimlessly around the city. According to our reports, which we compared in Nairobi, each of us heard the cars around 5 a.m. It could not have been any other vehicle because it was dangerous for anyone else to drive at night.

Maybe I stayed too long on the road before going into hiding, but I was anxious to cover a good distance.

156

35

A MAMBA SNAKE AND
MANY MORE HURDLES

I was somewhere between Nakawa and Kyambogo when I heard a car coming from Kampala behind me and heading towards Jinja. It was dawn and already bright. I turned off the road and stood some ten yards from its edge, so that the car would pass without seeing me, but to my surprise the car – a white Peugeot 504 – stopped by the point where I'd turned off. I waited for no explanation, I ran for my life. I cut corners and made sharp turns to confuse my followers. Finally I spotted a half-built house and hid myself.

The house was a red-brick construction that had reached roof level before being abandoned. Grass and bushes had grown inside and some trees were as tall as the house itself. I entered through the sitting-room window to leave neither trace nor trail at the door. I sat in one of the bedrooms and kept quiet. I suspected State Research boys were looking for me outside. Around 7.30 a.m. I heard a man asking a woman who was doing some cultivation in the vicinity of the house whether she had seen anyone running past there. She had not seen me because when I climbed into the house she had not yet arrived, but this so increased my fright I decided not to leave until very late at night.

Around 9 a.m. there was a welcome shower which, although it soaked me, washed away most of my prison smell, making it that much more difficult for police dogs to detect me. When the sun was warm enough I came out from under the bush to an open area still within the house to dry myself, but almost at once I heard a helicopter hovering not too far away. I retreated to my hiding place under the bush and lay flat on the ground. It needed little imagination to know the helicopter was looking for escaped prisoners. I left no sign of habitation in the room visible from the air.

While I wondered which of the two traps would catch me first, I heard distant gunshots and jumped to the conclusion that crippled Kasujja, as the most conspicuous, had been shot. Poor Kasujja, I mourned, his turn had come, he'd be suffering no more the way I was.

I began to feel hungry but had no idea when or where I'd find something to eat. Suddenly, looking straight ahead, I saw a big mamba snake coiling towards me. When it saw me it was obviously frightened and stopped, raising its head, motionless save for the flickering of its tongue. This was so frightful a sight I wished I'd remained in the cell with John Okech; the problems facing me now I felt were greater than any of his could be. The snake raised and lowered its head several times while I lay still, trusting it would mistake me for a piece of wood. I remembered our old village belief that snakes don't bite very young babies, no doubt because these can do them no harm. It's believed that aggressive snakes like cobras and mambas attack any moving object rather than permit a move against them. Finally it dropped its head, executed a sinuous right-angle turn, climbed the wall and went out. I was limp with relief but my heart continued to pump at high speed.

For several hours I was confined to the house. The night was moonlit until about 4 a.m. when I could at least leave my hiding place. I walked along the road for about two hours, then I again went into hiding. It wasn't easy to find a suitable place because the area was heavily built up. I thought I'd found a patch of elephant grass high enough for my purpose but shortly discovered it wasn't thick enough; I could hear passers-by talking.

I was hungry, thirsty and weak. This forced me out of the bush earlier than on my first night of freedom. I investigated the back of a row of houses and found some food in the dustbins. I had covered much more distance than the previous day. This encouraged me so much that I left my hide-out before dark. I realized I was near a small shopping area where an open-air market had been held. People were streaming home before dark and I mingled with them as a disguise. I followed two elderly men, one of them carrying a filled gunny-bag on his head. He complained to his friend about the unusually poor sales he'd had that day. Behind me was a barefoot middle-aged woman carrying a new medium-sized saucepan. I merged with the group remarkably well and maintained my pace so as not to break the pattern. A car came from behind us and as it approached closer we all gave way to it. It was an ancient blue Austin with full headlights dimly on. When it reached me the driver stopped and offered us a lift. I quickly scanned both driver and car to decide whether he might be a State Research boy, but he was a balding man of about sixty with grey hair. His bushy eyebrows were also grey. He wore a blue overall and had practically nothing in the car, which convinced me he couldn't belong to the notorious club of slaughterers.

I was exhausted and a lift would help me towards my objective. Wearily I climbed into the front passenger seat while he opened the back door for the woman to get in, thinking we were together. 'Won't your wife come, too?' he asked.

'Actually, although we've been walking together, she's not my wife,' I told him.

'That doesn't matter, she can still come in.' He turned to her and said, 'Madam, please step in, this is a free lift without any strings attached. Can't you see I'm too old for you to be afraid of me?' The woman didn't react, merely stood still waiting for the car to drive off. 'Please come in,' he invited her again. 'I won't eat you. I'm happy to help you because it's getting late for pedestrians.'

When he saw she was still uncomprehending and immovable, he closed the door and we set off. He started the conversation by asking where I worked. This took me by surprise because I was sure he had detected my prison smell and must be wondering where I'd come from. 'I work in the Ministry of Agriculture,' I invented, 'and I've been working on a farm for the last two days showing one of our progressive farmers the advantages of mixed farming. I've literally disposed of heaps and heaps of cow dung into his coffee plantation to demonstrate how easily he can obtain manure. You can probably detect the farm smell on me.'

'It's not that,' he said hastily. 'In fact I can't smell anything, but you're walking barefoot and that surprises me.'

'Well,' I brought out slowly while I thought furiously, 'my shoes were stolen on the farm, so I've had no choice.'

The conversation continued until he stopped to buy sugar, bread and milk, and when we resumed our journey, I asked him what his occupation was.

'I'm a police officer,' he replied. A police officer! I held my breath to show no surprise. Here is a plain-clothes policeman driving me to my death, I said to myself. How many hurdles would I have to clear before reaching safety? After escaping a deadly snake I wind up in a policeman's hands, voluntarily, too! It's too much, I thought. Realizing my attention had wandered he repeated what he had said and added that he was stationed at Naguru police station, which was feared for its reputation for torture and killings. 'We've been very busy today, that's why I'm so late in leaving!'

I wanted to change the topic but could think of nothing to say. We were following the old Kampala–Jinja road, in a sparsely populated area. It was night and certainly dangerous to walk alone but I could not bear the mental torture of his company an instant longer and told him I had to cut short my journey to see my wife's uncle.

'Where is he?'

'Here, we're just coming to it, sir,' I answered.

'You mean your uncle lives here in the bush where there isn't a sign of life?' he asked, astonished.

'That's right,' I said, trying to appear nonchalant. 'I used to live here when I was young so I know exactly where he is.'

'But there isn't even a house!' he protested.

'You can't see it from the road,' I told him. 'Actually there's a

160

path through the bush which leads to the small village where he lives.'

I insisted he stopped and that I'd be safe, and said goodbye as I stepped into pitch darkness not knowing where I really was. When I saw his red tail-lights disappear I let out a sigh of relief.

I'd avoided another trap! What hazards there were in escaping from prison – one perilous situation after another. Now I was faced with highway robbers and of course wild animals but these concerned me less than what might happen to me at the hands of my own kind. I was alone in a completely unknown place, surrounded by huge trees, and could hear only the shrill of bats. I rested half an hour before walking on.

As I'd now gained some confidence I walked for several days, sleeping at night in the bush. I had another two meals and some fruit. For the meals I concocted a story especially for old women: that I had been released from Mulago Hospital but that I had to walk back to my home in Jinja because I had no money. I let this sink in and then asked for food. I used the same story on an old man who gave me a pair of used trousers.

My biggest obstacle during those first two weeks was the River Nile. There are only two ways of crossing it: one is by the road bridge and the other by the rail one and at both soldiers checked on everyone. Initially I thought it best to use the rail but then decided against it as it would obviously point to my running away as no pedestrian uses that route. I hid in the bush for some days, planning how to cross.

On the second evening I overheard people returning from work in Jinja town rejoicing over the removal of some road blocks. 'The one remaining at the bridge is the usual one,' somebody said.

After our escape, Amin had placed road blocks all over the country in an effort to catch us, so it was interesting to learn that these had now beeen removed. I was later told that some outside radio stations were reporting that we had all made it to safety in neighbouring countries. This naturally displeased Amin but, due to public outcry, the additional road blocks had been removed.

'This road block is intended to catch coffee-smugglers,'

another voice said. After a burst of laughter, the same voice continued, 'Although Mr Big Daddy says he fears nothing except God, this time he's found someone else he should fear. He's been given a lesson! Can you imagine how prisoners could escape from his maximum-security jail and travel to Kenya without leaving a single trace? These sons of bitches – the Jews – are too clever for him.'

'I heard one radio report that some of them have already reached Germany,' someone else said.

'That's why he saw no point in further inconveniencing the travelling public,' the first voice replied. 'Anyway, those boys should be given credit because although their plan to topple Big Daddy failed, they succeeded in escaping from his slaughterhouse and that's more than anyone else has done!'

This was good news. I gathered up courage and decided to mix with the morning workers to cross the bridge the next day. My plan worked; I reached the other side of the river without incident and was now in Jinja.

My way through Busoga was relatively easy as I was now walking with confidence during the day. I preferred walking alone and avoided people. Being fluent in Lusoga, the local language, I could easily disguise myself. I modified my story after Jinja: I was now walking to my home town in Tororo, a town near the Kenya/Uganda border, from the hospital in Jinja. My story worked amazingly well and I made it to the border town of Busia, near Tororo, without difficulty.

Crossing the border was my next hurdle. During Amin's regime special clearance was required to leave the country. In order to implement this, the government had reinforced all points of exit with additional State Research boys. This determined my actions. I crossed the border through the bush, making sure no one saw me enter and avoiding any clearly marked path as Amin's anti-smuggler patrol might be on it. I headed steadily east until I calculated I was already well into Kenya. When I reached the road, shortly after noon, and established this was so I literally jumped for joy.

36

IN KENYA!

I felt I was now safe. It was again freedom, liberty and democracy for me. I was in a different world, a world where human rights are respected, a world where freedom of speech prevailed. The air had a spectacular taste; I felt I'd stepped into heaven where there is joy and justice for all.

I sat down by the roadside, trying to plan what to do with my freedom. I realized that being a Ugandan in Kenya was risky as the Kenyan authorities could repatriate me to Uganda. I realized, too, that I had no identity card, which was enough for me to be considered a vagrant and an undesirable character.

I stood up and began walking to Kisumu which I estimated to be about sixty-five miles distant. Having worked in both Kenya and Tanzania, I felt at home in Kenya and, furthermore, my Swahili was good and so was my knowledge of the tribes and local cultures, especially in western Kenya. I walked on with growing confidence, speaking to as many people as possible along the way, partly to brush up my Swahili and partly to maintain my confidence.

My first night in Kenya was spent in a jungle of short grass and, for the first time since my escape, I had to worry about mosquitoes, cold weather and wild animals. I had had nothing to eat for twenty-four hours and apart from shirt and trousers, nothing to protect me against the cold.

The following day was difficult because I was unsuccessful in begging for food. I found Kenyans less hospitable than Ugandans as, despite my stories of suffering, I won no sympathy from those whom I asked for assistance. My new story was that I was an employee of the East African Community working in the Research Institute on the Kenya side of the Kenya/Uganda border near Busia. I was on my way to Kisumu when thieves robbed me of all my belongings including my identity card. I asked for assistance to reach Kisumu where I could report to our offices. This story was to legalize my stay in Kenya and elicit sympathy.

By the end of the day I reached a small town where I scavenged for food in dustbins and found a hiding place for the night. The next morning I approached some Somalis whose patrol tanker had broken down and who gave me a hundred shillings which not only enabled me to buy food, but also paid for my fare to Kisumu. My journey to Kisumu was faster but not much easier because of several police road blocks. Fortunately for me, I sat at the front of the mini-bus together with a policeman bound for Nairobi. Whenever we were stopped for a check, I was skipped over because of the presence of this policeman.

I had polished up my Swahili to sound like that of a Kenyan and neither the policeman nor the driver doubted my story. The mini-bus stopped at Kisumu where my fare ended, my dinner was dustbin scraps as usual and then I retreated to the outskirts of town. I didn't want to stay with nightwatchmen because of the possibility of being mistaken for a thief.

My travel up to Kericho was uneventful; the days were long and the nights very cold. I reached Kericho thoroughly exhausted, my feet swollen and with a deep gash in my right foot. I developed a high temperature, most likely from malaria, and in despair went to the police station and asked to stay overnight but was chased away. I joined a group of nightwatch-men around a fire where I was accepted and, for the first time since escaping, I had a warm night. I also became friendly with some people who offered to look for transport to take me to Nairobi. The lorry found for me was going to Nakuru but the driver promised to locate another for me, Nairobi-bound. This lorry broke down fifteen miles from Kericho and I stayed there for two days before deciding to continue on my way by walking as the lorry had to be towed back to Kericho for repair. The driver gave me fifty shillings and wished me 'all the best'.

I travelled through Nakuru, Naivasha, the Rift Valley and finally Limuru. The most uncomfortable portion of this lap was up the escarpment where I feared a meeting with robbers. The sun was setting when I reached Kabete, the western suburb of Nairobi. Filled with joy at again being in Nairobi I treated myself to a bus from Kabete to the city centre with the one shilling remaining in my pocket. The fare was seventy cents. By 7.30 p.m. I was in the city centre from where I walked to Nairobi South 'C', my final destination, arriving at 8.45 p.m. The date was 30 October 1977.

When I knocked at the door of my friend's house, his wife was in the kitchen and he was upstairs taking a shower. Neither could hear the argument between me and the children who refused to let me in, convinced I was a thief. When the wife heard my voice she shrieked with joy as she had been told that I had been killed. She embraced me and then burst into tears. The husband rushed downstairs with only a towel around his hips, embraced me and asked me how I'd travelled to Nairobi.

A teapot of hot milk was immediately given to me and this I gulped as I ravenously ate buttered bread. I had my first bath in two months. I felt as if I were coming back to my own body again. We then sat down and I told them all that had happened. Everyone listened attentively, there was no other sound but my voice, and now and then an occasional question. My story sounded so unlikely it was difficult for them to accept it, the more so as they believed what they'd heard, that we had been set free by nameless high-ranking officers. It was 1 a.m. when supper was served and, although I was woefully tired, with eating and drinking and celebrating my escape, I didn't get to bed until 3.30 a.m.

When I was shown my well-made bed in a well-lit room full of sweet fresh air, my mind went back to the Nakasero cell. The bed had a thick, soft mattress, white sheets, a lamp at the bedhead and there was a carpet underfoot. My host had given me clean trousers, a shirt and sweater. My own trousers and shirt were boiled to kill the prison lice. I knelt by the bedside and prayed. I slept soundly that night and the next day visited my sister and another good friend who bought me a proper pair of trousers, a shirt and a tie and a pair of shoes.

I remained in hiding. Should Amin or his henchmen learn of my safe arrival in Nairobi, they would kill all my friends and relatives in Uganda in reprisal. My fears were not unfounded because immediately after our escape Sande had been arrested for having taken my message to my family. Mr Mukasa together with Mr Wamae were also arrested for having received the message. Surprisingly, my wife was not arrested. Mr Wamae was later released, but Mukasa and Sande were taken to the notorious Makindye Military Police Headquarters, where they met up with our former cell-mate, John Okech, who was being tortured there.

37

OKECH'S END

Life is too valuable to be relinquished easily and John Okech made two unsuccessful attempts to flee after our escape. He had finally made enough noise to attract the duty guards to come downstairs. His first story was that we had escaped while he was fast asleep. These guards were so frightened that they ran for their lives, knowing their superiors would not receive escape news with any warmth. Probably as a cover-up they acceded to Okech's request for a gun to kill himself with rather than undergo the imminent torture.

The next lot of guards came down around 6 a.m. There were six of them, all armed. They rushed to Okech's cell gate. Okech had worked out a scheme which almost saved him. With his automatic gun he methodically shot the six soldiers, threw his gun into the corridor where the soldiers' bodies were, put his handcuffs back on and waited. An hour later yet another group came down who were ignorant of our escape but the absence of security guards upstairs had alerted them to something odd within the prison. Arriving downstairs they were stunned to see the bodies of soldiers dead in the corridor with their guns flung about them. Okech immediately told them what had happened. 'Efendi, some white soldiers came down in the middle of the night, opened the cell and released all my cellmates whose names were on their list. They refused to take me with them because my name wasn't on the list.'

'What nationality were they?' one soldier asked.

'I don't know, *Efendi,*' Okech replied, 'but I thought they might be Israelis.'

This episode gave rise to the story I'd heard by the Nile bridge and, after the Entebbe raid, it was easily credited.

The report of our escape reached Amin in the Entebbe State House, disquieting news brought to him by Faruk Minawa. Amin was wild because of the humiliation brought to him by our escape. He said it was only fifteen months earlier that the Israelis had flown all the way from Tel Aviv to Entebbe Airport to rescue their fellow Israelis held as hostages by Palestinian soldiers. He claimed the same people had killed his soldiers guarding Naka-sero prison and taken away the 'presidential prisoners' he had anticipated killing by bazookas at the next firing squad.

'All the same,' he said, 'I put the blame on you and Colonel Itabuka.' He ordered the immediate arrest of Faruk Minawa, the removal of Colonel Itabuka from the State Research Bureau and the promotion of Captain Yoswa as new head of the bureau. 'Nevertheless,' he ordered, 'don't release him [meaning Okech] but take him back to his cell.' It was this afterthought that ruined Okech's plans. Okech had been brought before Amin to whom he told the story which was initially believed. Amin, intelligent and crafty, insisted on more facts about our escape despite the plausibility of the Israeli rescue story. To the surprise of his own soldiers and Okech's dismay, Amin ordered him to be returned to Cell 2, which was as good as being plunged into hell because the soldiers then saw the hole through which we'd escaped and it became obvious Okech had been telling lies. The discovery made Amin no happier, however, as he thought this could still be another trick. He transferred Okech to Makindye Prison for torture and also ordered the arrest of anyone suspected of having assisted us in our escape.

Mukasa, Sande and Okech were locked in one cell with hand-cuffs and long iron chains on their legs. Their cell was right beside the infamous go-down where prisoners were normally killed, a horrifying sight for them to witness. Sande frequently quarrelled with Mukasa, blaming him for his arrest which was

168

due to the message I'd given him. Mr Mukasa was accused of having paid a million US dollars as a bribe to Amin's soldiers to allow us to escape.

Although the three prisoners later became very close friends, Okech never disclosed our true story to either Mukasa or Sande. He maintained the official version that high-ranking Israeli soldiers had opened our cell and set us free. He did show them, however, our secret method for opening handcuffs and they were able to remove them at night, as we had done.

Okech was killed at Makindye after a month of torture, Sande was killed about four weeks later but, by the grace of God, after six months of torture Mr Mukasa was released.

Although most killings were done in the go-down, a few others took place outside the building. One VIP was killed while enjoying the afternoon sun after being let out of his cell for fresh air. A soldier hit him on the head with a wooden sledgehammer so that he died looking up, as if begging for mercy.

Mr Mukasa survived several attempts to kill him before Amin accepted his wife's plea, through an uncle of Amin's, to release her husband on the grounds that it was manifestly ridiculous to believe a mere civil servant could afford to spend a million US dollars to bribe soldiers for the release of a friend. I was relieved at the news; I didn't want Mukasa killed for allegedly saving me. Surprisingly, he elected to remain in Uganda after his release.

I remained in exile until after the fall of Amin. It is a terrible thing for a patriotic citizen to love his country and hate his government.

INDEX